A CENTURY OF SERVICE

THE PUGET POWER STORY

BY

Robert C. Wing

EDITOR

Robert C. Cumbow

ASSOCIATE EDITOR

Julie Springer

DESIGNER

PUBLISHED BY

Puget Sound Power & Light Company

10608 N.E. 4th Street   Bellevue, Washington 98004-5028

Publisher: *Neil L. McReynolds*

Contributing Writers: *Stewart G. Neel, James R. Warren,*
Michael B. Hunter, William S. Weaver

Editorial Board: *Bill Dudley, Robert W. Evans, Alden B. Couch,*
Keith A. Murray, Stewart G. Neel, Arthur Kramer,
Arthur H. McDonald, James R. Warren

Research Assistance: *Susan Ball*

Executive Editorial Secretary: *Clyde Margolis*

Design/Production/Publishing Coordinator: *Diana Maxum*

Photography Research: *Julie Springer, Patricia Treger, Patricia Plumb,*
Kim Gerde, Greg Dziekonski

Typesetting: *Maria Rash*

Contributing Artists: *Gary P. Nelson, Val Paul Taylor, Ron Bomba*

Photography Coordinator: *Charles Nishida*

Contributing Photographers: *Patricia Treger, Brian Morris*
Fred Boor, David Blythe,
David Watanabe

FIRST EDITION

Library of Congress Cataloging-in-Publication Data
A Century of service.
   Bibliography: p. 167
   Includes index.
   1. Puget Sound Power & Light Company — History.
2. Electric utilities — Northwest, Pacific — History.
I. Wing, Robert C., 1921-   . II. Cumbow, Robert C., 1946-
HD9685.U7P923   1987   338.7'6136362'097977   87-16582
ISBN 0-9619061-0-3

Printed in the United States of America.

The Stone & Webster
"Gang" during the
stringing of trans-
Cascade electric cables
across Stevens Pass in
1927. These lines were
a critical link between
Puget Power stations
on both sides of the
Cascades, at a time
when the young com-
pany was still building
its network under the
Stone & Webster aegis.

To the employees of
Puget Sound Power & Light Company
past, present and future,
this book is gratefully dedicated.

Acknowledgments

*I*n addition to the contributing writers, the editors are grateful to numerous individuals who contributed to this work in several ways. The Editorial Board met for a period of over a year providing guidance, conducting oral history interviews and reviewing the manuscript. The following individuals participated in interviews, reviewed the manuscript, provided the editors with specific insights on pivotal events or performed valuable historical or photographic research.

J. Harold Abramson

Jack A. Austin

Noel B. Bicknell

Lucius Biglow Jr.

Steve Blewett

Alfred A. Brandt

Wayne G. Bressler

Vincent O. Burns

Rick Caldwell

Mrs. Howard G.
   (Olive) Carter

Marian E. Cochran

Billie Dahl

Ralph M. Davis

Richard H. Engeman

Mrs. Francis H. Ferguson

David Freeh

Richard Frederick

M. E. (Gene) Galloway Jr.

Howard Giske

Patrick F. Hargreaves

Kennan E. Hollingsworth

Ann Hopping

Lawrence E. Karrer

John H. King

David H. Knight

Andrew B. Loft

Joseph Maguire

Carolyn Marr

John C. Micka

Lowell P. Mickelwait

Elaine Miller

Walton W. (Doc)
   Moreland

William A. Myers

Joseph M. Phillips

Raymond V. Pollard

Harry J. Prior

Wallace W. Quistorff

Wendell J. Satre

R. F. (Shep) Schaefer

Glen Simons

Edward T. Stone

Charles L. Vogel

Joy Werlink

Richard F. Whaley

Kay Wilson

Thomas A. Edison with some of his "Edison Effect" lamps. Edison's development of practical uses for electricity, combined with the later perfection of alternating current, made electric utilities a growth industry a century ago.

Courtesy of the Edison National Historic Site

Table of Contents

A turn-of-the-century line crew from the Seattle Electric Company. The company was one of dozens that, over a century, merged to form Puget Power.

Courtesy of the Museum of History & Industry

Preface

*T*homas Edison's invention of the incandescent lamp in 1879 opened the door for the practical application of electricity to homes and shops as well as industries. Public acceptance was immediate, and a whole new array of business opportunities were born. It is not surprising, then, that in 1987 many electric utility companies in the United States can trace their origins back about a hundred years. In western Washington, however, it is unusual for any company or institution to be able to claim that sort of durability. In 1885-87 Washington was still a territory, still completing the transition from a way station for adventurers and opportunists to a stable community of settlers and builders worthy of statehood.

The demonstrated durability of Puget Sound Power & Light is doubly remarkable in that it had to survive first the rigors of a frontier beginning, and later an adversarial political climate that was, on a national scale, uniquely threatening. But Puget Power did not just survive. It grew with the area it serves, to become the largest electric utility in the state of Washington. It continues to grow, adapting its services to the needs of customers and its operations to an ever-changing business climate. This survival and continuing growth is a credit to the tenacity, integrity, and dedication of its employees, past and present. To these individuals, this book is gratefully dedicated.

This story of Puget Power is not a chronological diary of dates, places and events. For those interested in that sort of detail, the volumes of data that an investor-owned, publicly-regulated utility must file with the State, the Securities and Exchange Commission, the Federal Energy Regulatory Commission, and other agencies, are readily available. In addition, a very workmanlike company documentary has been published: *Among the Live Wires* by Arthur Kramer, a long-time employee now retired.

A Century of Service tells the story of Puget Power in a different way, recounting pivotal events and critical situations through which the "corporate ship" has been navigated in the past. For those employees now retired, it should serve as one more reaffirmation of jobs well done. For those who are carrying on now, and still others who will complete the second "Century of Service," we hope this account will serve as an inspiration, as they read of the dedication to customers and investors that their predecessors have demonstrated.

Finally, we hope this account will be a permanent record of the colorful, action-packed drama of the electric utility business, and a lasting reminder of what we mean when we say: **The Energy Starts Here.**

Edison's first successful
incandescent lamp had
a filament of
carbonized cotton
sewing thread and
burned for 40 hours.

**Courtesy of the Edison
National Historic Site**

The Occidental Hotel,
where Mitchell and
Sparling spent their first
night in Seattle, domi-
nates this view of Mill
Street (now Yesler
Way), as downtown
Seattle looked before
the 1889 fire.

**Courtesy of the
U of W Libraries**

CHAPTER 1
In the beginning there was light

With a whish-woosh of its quiet steam engine, the passenger boat *Emma Hayward* from Tacoma nudges into the wharf at the foot of Jackson Street. End of voyage: Seattle. The late-day sky is gray, and a light rain is falling — summer has ended ... the summer of 1885.

Two young men stride the short gangway to the wharf, retrieve their hand baggage, and make their way through the drizzle to the small ticket room at the street end. Their taut expressions and rumpled clothes evidence the strains of the week-long trip from New York City, but they walk with military bearing that is by now second nature.

After checking directions with the station clerk, they head three blocks north on Commercial Street and one block east on Yesler to the Occidental Hotel. The ankle-deep mud is a reminder that, for all its well-publicized growth momentum, Seattle is still a territorial frontier town. Another reminder: A gas lamp lights the registration desk in the hotel lobby. And as our two travelers sign in, Sidney Z. Mitchell and F. H. Sparling tell themselves that the lamp is something they mean to change — in a big way.

These two young-men-in-a-hurry were up with the clammy October dawn and off to survey Seattle prospects. The Seattle they saw that morning was moving through the period that historian Edmond S. Meany has called the (1879-1889) "turbulent decade." The city was suffering the growing pains of adolescence. From a population of under 4,000 in 1880, that growth had accelerated until, to the surprise of many, it surpassed Port Townsend, Olympia, and Walla Walla. With population approaching 10,000 in 1885, Seattle was the metropolis of the territory.

Looking about, Mitchell and Sparling saw a town that had kept expanding block by block over the hills to the east, north and south, dodging the steepest slopes — such as the southern flank of Denny Hill — and the mudflats at the base of Beacon Hill, two hindrances to growth that the city would remove within two decades.

The old town on Doc Maynard's spit showed its frontier roots: Simple wooden structures with a few brick facades and false fronts overlooked muddy streets. But where business was expanding to the north, newer, higher structures dominated. High on First Hill, a few fine homes could

Edison listening to his improved wax cylinder phonograph, June, 1888. Edison was pioneering new uses for electric power while his affiliates were busy promoting the revolutionary new energy source.

Courtesy of the Edison National Historic Site

Above left: *Ornate but cumbersome and inefficient gas and oil lamps became obsolete when Edison proteges such as Sidney Z. Mitchell began marketing electric lighting systems.*

The Emma Hayward brought Mitchell and Sparling to Seattle in 1885.

Photo by Asahel Curtis
Courtesy of the Museum of History & Industry

Downtown Seattle, 1897, from the corner of Front Street (later 1st Avenue) and Main. In this neighborhood, the offices of Mitchell & Sparling were established in 1885. The San Francisco store, visable on the right, later housed the area's first generator. In the background, the scene is dominated by the University of Washington, Central School, and the Frye Opera House.

Photo by Asahel Curtis
Courtesy of the
Washington State
Historical Society

be seen. From Elliott Bay, three pinnacles of progress crowned the town: the just-completed Frye Opera House, the University of Washington (built in 1861), and the new Central School (built in 1882), a large four-story white wooden building with a clock tower. The last burned to the ground a couple of years later, and was replaced by a larger brick school.

The progress Mitchell and Sparling saw in Seattle to date was all the more remarkable for having been accomplished without a railroad connection to the rest of the country. The Northern Pacific Railroad, several years earlier, had been extended west to Portland, Oregon and north to its terminus in Tacoma. A branch line was further extended

to Seattle in 1883; but after brief operation, service had been halted in 1884.

Beneath the surface appearance of flourishing business were several social and political tensions. Newcomers were arriving in numbers that exceeded the jobs available even from the expanding extractive industries — lumber, coal, salmon fishing, and agriculture. Resentment was rising over the number of Chinese, earlier imported as railroad laborers,

Below: Chinese immigrants helped build railroads into the Northwest and founded the Seattle area's Asian community.

Courtesy of the
U of W Libraries

now willing to work at substandard wages. A now-aging early pioneer and former mayor, Henry Yesler, had been prevailed upon to serve another one-year term.

The greatest stimulus for growth was the promise of a future without the problems of isolation. Seattle was about to gain access to the rest of the country. By the end of the decade, Seattle would become a major railroad terminus. The rails would soon be carrying tens of thousands of immigrants each year to the Puget Sound country, and over the same rails increasing amounts of Northwest products would flow eastward to distant markets.

By the end of that first day, Mitchell and Sparling had rented office space at 629 Front Street. They were in business as the Northwest

Henry Yesler was Seattle's first mayor and presided at the area's first display of electric lighting.

Courtesy of the Museum of History & Industry

Regional Agents for the Edison Electric Light Company.

Sidney Z. Mitchell was born in Dadeville, Alabama during the War Between the States, March 17, 1862. He was given the middle name Zollicoffer, for a popular confederate general who had fallen at the battle of Mill Creek the previous January. An outstanding student, Mitchell had been admitted by examination to the U.S. Naval Academy, from which he was graduated in 1883. At that time, graduate officer candidates

were required to serve two years at sea before being granted a commission. Sidney Mitchell's tour took him to the Mediterranean for most of that period. During engineering classes at the Academy his attention had been attracted to reports of the progress Thomas Edison was making in developing electric lighting. Sensing immedi-

Above: Sidney Z. Mitchell in 1893.

The A. A. Denny was Seattle's first locomotive, operating between Seattle and Renton before electric power made possible the interurban transit system.

Courtesy of the U of W Libraries

ately the great improvement this could make in working and living quarters in the dank, dark compartments of a ship, Mitchell obtained permission to install experimental systems during his tour of sea duty. When his tour was completed in early 1885, the U.S. Navy was in the midst of a major cutback. Mitchell, his classmate Sparling, and most of their contemporaries had to find other employment.

Mitchell quickly made his way to Thomas Edison's laboratories at the Pearl Street Station in New York City. There, after an interview with the great Edison himself, he was hired and enrolled in the concentrated classes being conducted for engineers from throughout the world who were coming to learn the special skills necessary to design and install lighting, generating and switching equipment.

Mitchell soon made a favorable impression on Edison. After six months at Pearl Street, and at the age of 23, he was appointed exclusive agent for the Edison Electric Light Company, covering the State of Oregon and the territories of Washington, Montana and Alaska. Adventure and a new career were opening up for this bright young man: He grabbed his buddy Sparling and headed West. The adventure would come soon; the career would carry him beyond his wildest dreams.

From the Spartan office at 629 Front Street, Mitchell & Sparling Company, with Mitchell in the lead,

launched a promotional campaign that was to be the model for the development of electric service utilities throughout the territory in years to come. For sheer energy and enthusiasm it could also have been the model for the River City "Music Man" of Broadway fame decades later.

Lighting Up Seattle

Step one was a meeting with the mayor. Mitchell and Sparling enthusiastically described the advantages to all citizens of the light provided by the new incandescent electric bulb, with special emphasis on the advantage to the mayor, who would lead his city into a new era. They sought the mayor's counsel on which local citizens should be invited to head a new company to develop the system. By the end of October, the Seattle Electric Light Company was formed. The founding officers were George D. Hill, President; James Frink, Vice President and Superintendent. Mitchell and Sparling were modestly identified as "electricians."

By November, the mayor and the City Council had granted the company the 25-year franchise deemed necessary to permit and justify the investment in poles, wire

Edison's laboratories were located in the famous Pearl Street Station in New York City. It was here that Sidney Z. Mitchell acquired the expertise that made him the Northwest's first marketer of electricity.

Courtesy of the Edison National Historic Site

and the generating plant. In February 1886, work started on the foundations for the boiler, steam engine and generator off Jackson Street between First Avenue South and Occidental Avenue.

Finally, on March 22, 1886, came the moment of truth; the great demonstration to "prove up" on the franchise. At the company's headquarters an array of eleven 16-candle-power lamps were positioned around a meeting room, and one 30-candle-power lamp was mounted over the street entrance. Amid a gala gathering of the mayor, council and local dignitaries, and upon a signal to the "fired up" boiler crew, the dynamo was started. A Post-Intelligencer reporter wrote that, "When the dynamo was started, instantly the room was made brilliant with a clear white light!"

The crowd reacted as if a set of 4th of July rockets had burst before their eyes. And as the company president and the mayor congratulated each other at the center of the delighted throng, off to one side the two young "electricians" exchanged smiles of satisfaction. Their first sale of Edison equipment had been well received. That their future success was assured seemed clear. What could not be clear at that moment was that the Seattle Electric Light Company, spawned by their efforts, would grow, survive crisis after crisis, and combine with other budding utility operations to become Puget Sound Power & Light Company.

They had launched the first Puget Power "Century of Service."

Following the demonstration, the initial system was quickly expanded to 250 lamps. It was the first central station system for incandescent electric lighting west of the Rocky Mountains.

Building on his success in Seattle, Mitchell rapidly expanded his operations. In 1886 he built a small hydro plant in Spokane. Over the next 15 years he organized and built steam-powered central station systems in Tacoma, Portland, Bellingham and many smaller towns in Washington, Oregon, Idaho, and British Columbia.

Mitchell was not alone in expand-

7

ing the use of electricity in the Northwest. The appeal and applications of incandescent lighting were immediate and far-reaching. But as uses for electricity grew, a growing list of problems emerged — technical, operational, financial, political, and legal problems for which prior industrial experience was of only limited benefit. Many of these problems would test this new industry for years to come — some to the present day. The challenge was at hand. The stakes, for individuals and organizations, were nothing short of survival.

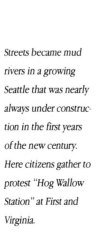

Streets became mud rivers in a growing Seattle that was nearly always under construction in the first years of the new century. Here citizens gather to protest "Hog Wallow Station" at First and Virginia.

Courtesy of the U of W Libraries

Snoqualmie Falls
before Charles Baker;
August, 1890.

Photo by F. Jay Haynes
Courtesy of
the Montana
Historical Society

Coal mines like this
one near Renton were
among the first indus-
trial customers of
fledgling electric
companies.

Photo by Asahel Curtis
Courtesy of the
Washington State
Historical Society

The thrill of victory – the agony of defeat

While Sidney Mitchell was busy developing central station electricity systems in the populous centers of western Washington, many more "shirt tail" systems were appearing in the villages and byways. The incandescent bulb was the immediate answer to extending the operating hours of the many lumber mills around Puget Sound. Since these mills already had steam power, the addition of a dynamo to generate electricity was relatively simple. The same was true of the coal mines at Newcastle in King County, at Bellingham and in Kittitas County; and of the food processing plants in the Skagit Valley and in Chelan.

Typically a housing area (often company-owned) was located adjacent to each of these plants. Quickly a power line would be extended from the mill down the main wagon road, so that each house or bunkhouse could have a lamp. Just as quickly the mill found itself in the utility service business — not always to its liking.

So appealing were the benefits of electricity that the demand for more seemed without limit. In increasing numbers these village systems were organized as independent electric utilities. They were subject to the fortunes of an unregulated and occasionally fiercely competitive market, and joined the city systems in confronting several generic industry problems.

A relatively high initial investment

was required for a system to serve a load limited to lights used only a few hours a day. Field operations were complicated by the difficulty of obtaining franchises and permits for power lines, in the face of limited public understanding and even fear of this new technology. (Seattle Electric Co. was asked why it did not locate its dynamos at the top of the hills "so the power could run downhill rather than being pumped up," and one citizen complained of being injured from exposure to the glaring arc from a loose street-car trolley.)

Then there was the serious challenge of financing system growth. Major additions could not be paid for with current revenues, and neither new investment capital nor credit for borrowing was readily available to a new high-tech enterprise with no history of success. And

finally, after the initial dynamo capacity was exceeded, where would the additional power supply be found? Would each small isolated lighting or streetcar system continue to add more dynamos and boilers, or would separate generating companies be formed to supply power

Electric power revolutionized the food processing industry.
Courtesy of the Washington State Historical Society

A souvenir of the power company Charles Baker built around his hydro project at Snoqualmie Falls.

under contract to several systems? In the late 1880s the technology to handle long-distance transmission of power and system interconnections was still under development.

Meeting the Challenges

How did Puget Power and its predecessor companies meet these challenges? Many of the solutions were (and continue to be) unique innovations subsequently adopted by other companies and regions.

For cities large enough to support streetcar systems (e.g., Seattle, Tacoma, Bellingham, Olympia), the electrification of these lines in the late 1880s broadened the base of electric system load beyond mere lightbulbs. However, these were not citywide systems but isolated com-

panies for each route (12 or more in Seattle), often built and subsidized to enhance the sale of suburban real estate developments. The travails of the streetcar chapter of Puget Power history still lay ahead.

As for the perennial challenge to provide the power supply for future load growth, the story of Snoqualmie Falls Plant No. 1, conceived by Charles Baker, could be the role model for that television sports catch-phrase, "the thrill of victory and the agony of defeat."

Baker's Dream

The Cornell University class of 1886 included Charles Hinckley Baker, who was graduated with honors as a civil engineer. For a young engineer the technical and romantic challenge of the day was to be found in pushing the rail

A one-block electric trolley to Washington Hotel atop Seattle's Denny Hill, before the 1907 regrade leveled the hill.

Courtesy of the Museum of History & Industry

transportation system over the western horizon to the Pacific shores of the rapidly growing nation. Charles Baker was a man of action. He headed west.

New as the adventure was for Charles, his trek to Seattle was also the symbolic completion of a journey started 25 years earlier by his father. In 1861 William Taylor Baker had left his home in upstate New York, intent on making his fortune in the west. Chicago was as far west as his meager resources would take

Charles Hinckley Baker.

him, but that didn't prevent him from making a fortune. His first job was clerk with a commission grain broker. He progressed rapidly from clerk to trader, to principal of the firm, to head of his own company. In 1890 he was elected President of the Chicago Board of Trade, and in 1891 he was named President of the Chicago Columbian World Exposition.

Charles Baker also made a stop on his way west: to work for the Chicago Northwestern Railway in the Dakota Territory. But after a year he moved on. In Seattle he went to work for the Seattle, Lake Shore & Eastern Railroad, which was building northward from Seattle to the Canadian border and eastward across the Cascade Mountains to Spokane. The latter line passed close by the great Snoqualmie Falls cataract, then regarded as an attraction mainly for fishermen and tourists.

Charles, whose work frequently took him past the site, saw an untapped resource. He began to formulate a plan to harness the power of that 270-foot fall of water. Slowly, meticulously and very privately, he developed solutions to the many problems he could forsee. Premature presentation of such a scheme would surely be dismissed as the impractical dreams of a crackpot. The reliability of an electricity supply generated by a seasonally variable water flow was not then well regarded. Even more critical was the question of long-distance transmission (40 miles!), still a subject of theoretical

The falls were a draw even before Baker's wonder, as this page from the 1895-6 Seattle directory attests.

Courtesy of the U of W Libraries

study and research by eminent scientist Nikola Tesla.

After three years on the railroad engineering job, Charles Baker resigned to open his own consulting engineering practice in Seattle. Success came rapidly in the high-growth era of 1890, and the addition of contracting services to his business proved even more profitable. In 1891 Baker contracted to build the Third Street and Suburban Electric Railway in Seattle for David Denny and associates. The work was just about completed when the financial panic of 1893 devastated Seattle and the nation. David Denny suffered complete financial failure in all of his numerous business ventures. Baker was only one of Denny's many associates who fell like dominoes, winding up with virtually no assets and $60,000 in unpaid judgments hanging over his head.

But that head remained clear — thinking through the bleak two years that followed. Amid the chaos Baker saw opportunity. If the eight or ten main streetcar lines, all bankrupt, could be consolidated, the electrical load would form just the revenue base needed to make his still active dream of a Snoqualmie Falls power generating plant feasible.

Baker obtained an option to buy the key property at Snoqualmie Falls and all but one of the street car lines in Seattle. Then, for the first time since his financial troubles began, he traveled to Chicago and laid the plan before his now wealthy father.

Demonstrating great confidence in his son's judgment and workmanship, Baker senior authorized Charles to proceed. They concurred that their agreement to undertake the project as equal partners would be undocumented and kept secret. Title to all real estate, water rights and equipment assets would be taken in the father's name only, to protect them from the reach of the judgments that still plagued Charles.

Construction of the Snoqualmie Falls plant proceeded in 1898 according to plan. The consolidation of the streetcar lines did not. The one line for which Baker had been unable to get an option now belonged to a group that included the General Electric Company and was headed by S. Z. Mitchell. Mitchell had also seen the advantage in consolidating all of Seattle's streetcar lines and was

Above: Names of the great pioneers of electricity adorned the upper end of the elevator.

Below: Visitors could stroll and marvel at the powerhouse carved from solid rock.

Above: An artist's diagram of the Snoqualmie project's head works.

Right: A construction crew at work on the intake during December 1898.

aggressively competing to achieve that end on his own terms. Ultimately Mitchell prevailed, but Baker proceeded with the Snoqualmie Falls plant, determined to market the power, if not in Seattle, then to Tacoma and Everett.

The plant was truly a marvel—the proverbial "eighth wonder," some said. A few key dimensions will help those who have not visited the site appreciate its unique features. About 500 feet back from the crest of the falls, part of the river is diverted downward through its bed, via an excavated shaft 10 x 28 feet. At the level of the lower river this shaft abruptly turns horizontally toward the foot of the falls, and expands into a large chamber 200 feet long, 40 feet wide, and 30 feet high — all excavated out of solid rock. This is the power house, in which were originally installed four great water wheels and generators capable of delivering a total of 6,000 kilowatts. The water, after passing down the shaft through two eight-foot wrought-iron penstocks and discharging through the water wheels, escapes through a tunnel about 400 feet long, likewise excavated through solid rock to the foot of the falls.

A solution to the power transmission problem was emerging from Westinghouse research: an alternating current system of transformers, an improvement over the Edison direct current scheme. This, and the adversary relationship that had evolved between Baker and the

15

The observation deck at Snoqualmie Falls: Charles Baker (center, in straw hat) entertains guests.

Dorothy Baker: As an infant, she pulled the switch that started the Snoqualmie project.

Right: The tailrace at Snoqualmie powerhouse.

Mitchell/General Electric interest, resulted in Westinghouse's supplying essentially all of the Snoqualmie Falls plant generating system. The transmission cable was aluminum with a hemp core. Power was initially transmitted at 32,000 volts, to substations in Seattle (32 miles), Tacoma (44 miles), Everett (36 miles), and several intervening small towns.

Construction was completed in remarkable time and at a cost per kilowatt of from one-third to one-half that of comparable plants of the day, and one-quarter that of Niagara Falls. The plant began producing power in 1898, with equally favorable operating costs. But the most telling mark of excellence is that in 1987, 88 years after start-up, the original generators are still producing their rated output of 6,000

kilowatts. In 1905 a fifth unit generating 5,600 kw was added. Still later, in 1910, a second power house was added just downstream on the opposite bank of the river. Total project capacity of 44,000 kw was finally attained in 1957.

In a special ceremony on July 31, 1899, Charles Baker held his one-year old daughter Dorothy gently in his arms and helped her tiny hand turn the "start up" switch. He had every reason to take pride in this accomplishment. But he was unable to turn pride to profit. Lacking the Seattle streetcar market he had planned for, Baker had to scramble for sales. The industry was yet unregulated. Competition was

The second power-house added to the Snoqualmie Falls project in 1910.

Snoqualmie Falls Power Co. operations staff. Charles Baker by the door.

Charles H. Baker.

fierce, including all manner of political intrigue and such frontier refinements as occasionally burning down a few of the competitor's poles. Baker was a first-rate engineer, but a "John Wayne" he wasn't. He had difficulty overcoming the objection, circulated by Mitchell and others, that the power supply he was offering was not reliable. He stumbled on to the losing side of a political battle over who would supply Tacoma's power.

But the cruelest blow of all came from faraway Chicago. Upon the death of his father, the estate administrator, whom Charles suspected of collusion with adversary financial interests, refused to accept any evidence or claim of his silent partnership interest in the Snoqualmie Falls Power Company. These assets were liquidated in settling the estate, and later were acquired by Stone & Webster, ultimately to become part of Puget Power. After a brief involvement with the White River hydroelectric project [see Chapter 5], Charles Baker retreated in defeat from the Washington state competitive arena to rebuild his fortunes later in the southeastern part of the country.

The dream realized: The Snoqualmie Falls transformer house, intake and elevator shaft housing, circa 1900.

CHAPTER 3

Stone & Webster: Charge!

Above: The team of Charles A. Stone and Edwin S. Webster, on their way to becoming a household word.
Right: The "nickel ride" was important to early Seattle streetcar-riders.

Horse-drawn streetcars first appeared in Seattle in 1884 though they had been a feature of eastern cities for several decades. The hilly terrain of Seattle threw a wrinkle into the expected operating economics of this equipment—one horse couldn't pull the load. With two horses the oats consumed per passenger-seat-mile rendered the operation unprofitable at the accepted (and expected) nickel fare.

This challenge led to Seattle's becoming one of the first American cities to have electrified streetcars. Interest in converting from horse-power to electric power started shortly after the introduction of incandescent lighting by the Seattle Electric Light Co. in 1886. With the leadership of Frank Osgood, a developer from Boston, and Dr. E. C. Kilbourne, a Seattle dentist, the first service was initiated on the morning of March 31, 1889 — to the utter amazement of customers and observers. Bystanders searched for the source of power, a curiosity summed up by a recently arrived Chinese resident with the colorful comment, "No pushee no pullee, just go like hellee!" Skeptics opined that the cars would never run in the rain because that "electricity stuff" would obviously be washed off the trolley cable.

The drive motors were products of the Thomson-Houston Company,

E.C. Kilbourne, the founder of the Pacific Electric Light Co.

later to become part of the General Electric Company. The advantages of serving lighting and streetcar power loads on a combined system were immediately obvious. Dr. E. C. Kilbourne, who seems to have had more interest in filling business opportunities than teeth, formed the Pacific Electric Light Co. in 1890 to do just that — thereby starting another of the family of companies that would become Puget Power. At the same time similar predecessor companies were being formed in Tacoma and in Bellingham.

Quickly a relatively large number of isolated companies and systems developed, serving combinations of lighting, power and streetcar loads in limited territories (12 or more in Seattle alone). Many of these were started by real estate developers who had little interest in — and even less talent for — the stern demands of a utility service enterprise. The nationwide financial panic of 1893 plunged nearly all of these companies into bankruptcy. Some of the companies continued to operate under court-appointed trustees, but the exciting young electric utility industry was stalled — on all of its tracks.

Calling S&W

A rescue operation of major proportions was called for. No one understood this better than Sidney Mitchell, who had been instrumental

Seattle streetcars were horsedrawn beginning in 1883. The first, shown here at Occidental and Yesler, on a special trip for the system's developers, the mayor, and several city officials. The city's steep hills required extra horses, and it was the burden of double oats and upkeep that soon led to the development of electric street railways as an economic alternative.

the day they took the entrance examinations for the Massachusetts Institute of Technology in 1884. Both signed up for the pioneer course in electrical engineering. They became so closely associated in their interests that even during college, friends referred to them as "Stone & Webster." After collaborating on a thesis titled *The Efficiency of Alternating Current Transformers,* they were graduated in 1888. Their goal to form a consulting engineering partnership was briefly thwarted by a respected professor who advised that there would not be enough business to support two electrical engineers in Boston. During the next year Stone was employed by the Thomson Electric Welding Company and later as agent for the C.R.C. Motor Company. Webster went to work for the investment banking firm of Kidder Peabody and Company where his father was a partner.

In 1889, with their confidence and determination renewed, they

launched the partnership of Stone & Webster. From a beginning practice of consulting engineering, their scope of activities rapidly expanded to include contract construction of electrical structures, building hydro power plants, and erecting streetcar systems. In less than ten years they were being called in to advise or operate troubled electric utilities and to participate in the financing, refinancing or acquisition of these same systems. Their professional reputation and contacts in the New England financial community enabled them to bring together reorganized utilities and new investment capital to the advantage of all parties.

So when Charles Stone, at the insistence of Sidney Mitchell and others, answered the call to Seattle in 1898, he arrived with a broad base of experience and a variety of resources. What he found was a mess: an array of small companies, all with rundown, poorly maintained equipment, each in some financial

in starting many of these now-defunct systems and whose operations now extended throughout the Northwest. Through his industry connections he knew that a likely direction to aim the call-to-quarters was toward an aggressive young firm in Boston.

Charles Augustus Stone and Edwin Sibley Webster became acquainted

Above: A steam shovel at Campbell's Crossing in 1910 during the building of the White River hydro plant.
Right: "Open model" car used for summer-time comfort on the Fairhaven and New Whatcom Railway's Lake Whatcom line, circa 1900.

bind, increasingly unable to serve the needs of a growing population and industrial base. Clearly, complete utility industry reorganization was essential — starting in Seattle and proceeding to the entire Puget Sound area. But reorganization alone would not be enough. The critical requirement was strong, tested, locally respected leadership. It didn't take Stone long to find his man.

Furth

Jacob Furth had emigrated from central Europe to California in 1856 at the age of 16. Beginning as a clothing store clerk while he learned the English language, he progressed to store manager, then to owner. Frugal living allowed him to save much of his income. Attracted by news of growing opportunities in Seattle — and after securing the financial support of San Francisco associates — Furth moved north in 1882 and started Puget Sound National Bank. When a merger with Seattle National Bank was negotiated in 1893, Furth became its president. During this same period he had served as a member of the city council for six years and was president of the Chamber of Commerce for two years. His reputation as a capable and fair banker had continued to grow as he worked to help his customers survive the panic of 1893. This experience deepened his interest in the financial problems of the struggling electric utilities and streetcar companies of the Puget Sound region.

Above: Stone &
Webster: Legends
in their own time.

*Electric trolley car at
the entrance to Seattle's
Woodland Park,
Fremont Avenue at
North 50th Street,
in the 1890s.*

**Courtesy of the
U of W Libraries**

Charles Stone persuaded Jacob
Furth to become president of the
newly-formed Seattle Electric Company in 1900. Initially this enterprise
consolidated under unified operation the properties of virtually all
the surviving lighting, traction, and
related subsidiary businesses in
Seattle. Stone & Webster were to faci-
litate the recapitalization of the new
company and to provide technical
services and operations consulting.

This was a milestone. Under Jacob
Furth's capable leadership, the
interests of the company continued
to expand throughout the Puget
Sound region, leading toward
incorporation in 1912 as the Puget
Sound Traction, Light and Power
Company. For Stone & Webster it
was the beginning of an important
business affiliation that would
endure formally for the next 43 years
and informally for nearly 20 more.

25

The Leschi Park- Lake
Washington cable car
in downtown Seattle
during the early years
of the century.

**Courtesy of the Museum
of History & Industry**

Interurban car made by
the Niles Car Co. of
Ohio, shown here in
1910 at Colby and Wall
in downtown Everett,
bound for Seattle. Odd-
numbered cars were
southbound. Note the
Everett Herald building
in the background.

CHAPTER 4

Riding the Iron Horse: Till the cars come home

The electric street railway and the interurban railway, critical ventures for the Northwest's young electric utility industry, had a tremendous impact on the Puget Sound region for about 40 years, from 1890 to 1930.

The work of yet another young Annapolis graduate, Frank J. Sprague, led to the creation of successful American electric railways. After five years of naval service, Sprague went to work as an assistant to Thomas A. Edison. He designed and built the Richmond Union Passenger Railway in Virginia. Practically all subsequent lines built in North America were based on his original patents.

The introduction of electrified streetcars to Seattle [see Chapter 3] spurred interest among businessmen in settlements on Bellingham Bay — Whatcom, New Whatcom and Fairhaven. A group of prominent citizens from Whatcom and New Whatcom, headed by Eugene Canfield and P. B. Cornwall, incorporated the Bellingham Bay Electric Street Railway. They contracted for equipment from the Thomson-Houston Company. A line was built along State Street from Beech to

*For much of the information and phraseology in this chapter, the editors acknowledge a debt to **The Electric Railway Era in Northwest Washington, 1890-1930**, by Daniel E. Turbeville III, Occasional Paper #12, Center of Pacific Northwest Studies, Western Washington University, Bellingham, Washington, 1978.*

Holly, then along Holly and 13th Street (now "C" Street) to West Street. A trial run was made at 1:00 a.m. on March 28, 1891, and regular service began the next day.

A competitor, the Fairhaven Street Railway, soon emerged with a line built up Harris Street from the Dock to 21st Street. The first car ran on October 19, 1891 and was so full of enthusiastic riders that it required three attempts to reach the top of Harris Street hill. In 1892 the Fairhaven Street Railway acquired new holdings, and by June the entire Bellingham Bay line was leased to the Fairhaven and New Whatcom.

The "Panic of 1893" began a decline in revenues that resulted in bankruptcy on March 20, 1896. The principal creditor was the General Electric Company of New York, successor to the firm of Thomson-Houston, which had built all of the original equipment.

General Electric, with Sidney Zollicoffer Mitchell as its agent, purchased the Fairhaven and New Whatcom for $75,000. Business improved, and the line began to make money and buy new equipment.

When the Stone & Webster Corporation of Boston entered the field, they acquired and merged Seattle Electric and several other small street railways to form the Seattle Electric Company. In 1902 they purchased the Fairhaven and New Whatcom Railway and several other companies in Whatcom County, reorganizing them into Whatcom County Railway and Light.

Waiting for the Interurban

During the first decade of the 20th Century, Stone & Webster began planning and building an interurban electric railway system that would link all the local systems from Bellingham to Tacoma. They hoped for a system reaching from Vancouver, British Columbia to Olympia.

Henry Bucey incorporated the Seattle-Tacoma Interurban on February 18, 1891, financed by Kidder Peabody and Company of

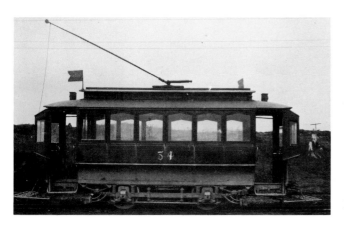

A Fairhaven-New Whatcom Railway streetcar, single-truck variety, manufactured by the J.G. Brill Co.

Courtesy of the U of W Libraries

Boston. While the line was under construction Bucey sold out to Seattle Electric Company, which incorporated the line as the Puget Sound Electric Railway on December 5, 1902. At the formal opening, the big, green Brill cars were filled with mayors, county officials, business dignitaries and railroad officials. The fare between Seattle and Tacoma was 60 cents one way and a dollar round trip.

Puget Sound Electric Railway also owned and operated the Tacoma street railway system. In 1908 PSE provided new service between Tacoma and Puyallup. PSE operated by an electrified third rail (instead of a trolley cable) from The Meadows Race Track (now Boeing Field) to Tacoma city limits, a distance of 28.15 miles. Overhead trolley wires served the remainder of the system.

From Roland Covey, electric railway historian:

Early in the 20th Century my parents came to Auburn to live. When the PSE line was first opened to traffic the fencing on the right-of-way had not been completed . . . A neighbor's bull wandered on the track, sniffed at the third rail and got quite a jolt. This aggressive animal then made another lunge at the third rail, only to be electrocuted.

From Harold Hill, PSE electric railway historian:

I have stood on the platform of the station on the trestle at Renton Junction and heard, saw and felt those green titans roar past at 40 miles an hour.

Many a businessman sat on the edge of his seat in a PSE smoker and watched the Milwaukee "Olympian"

on a parallel track racing neck-and-neck with his interurban train to maintain its schedule. PSE had to, and did, roll better than 60 miles per hour. Any train entering this stretch of track between Renton Junction and Kent, be it Union Pacific, Great Northern Railway, Northern Pacific, or Milwaukee, was automatically challenged to race by any interurban in the vicinity. Passengers laid bets on who would win.

An interurban line from Seattle to Everett was begun by Fred Sander, a Seattle real estate promoter. He had built from Seattle to Lake Ballinger when he sold out to Stone & Webster in 1907. The Seattle-Everett line was completed and opened on May 1, 1910.

On May 18, 1910 Stone & Webster incorporated the Bellingham and Skagit Interurban Railway. Franchises were granted immediately by Mount Vernon, Burlington and Sedro-Woolley. Bellingham held out, finally granting a franchise with several conditions, including one that the line must be completed to the south city limits by July 1, 1911. Stone & Webster accepted the conditions but in return required that local citizens subscribe $400,000 to the project. This was done.

Work began on November 10, 1910 with a number of Boston executives present at the ceremonial driving of a "golden spike" at the foot of Bellingham's McKenzie Street — at the beginning, not the completion, of construction. It was declared to be a half-holiday in Bellingham and thousands turned out for the event.

The first section built was a 4.3-mile segment from downtown Bellingham to the south city limits. Chuckanut Creek had to be bridged; the bridge was 700 feet long and 130 feet high. It was completed June 1, 1911, a month ahead of schedule.

Pushing on toward Skagit County, the crew encountered the next big obstacle — the stretch from Clayton Bay to Blanchard. Since the Great Northern Railroad had constructed its line there in 1902, it occupied the only available right-of-way along the base of Chuckanut Mountain's rocky shoreline. Stone & Webster "went to sea," building a four-mile trestle over salt water along the shore of Samish Bay that consumed 500 cedar piles and three million feet of lumber. The final big challenge was a bridge across the Skagit River, built in seven months and finished ahead of schedule.

At the driving of the Golden Spike for the Bellingham-Skagit Interurban Railroad, Bellingham, Wash, Nov. 10th, 1910.

In January 1912 when Stone & Webster incorporated the Puget Sound Traction, Light & Power Company, the Bellingham & Skagit was merged with Seattle-Everett Interurban to form the Pacific Northwest Traction Company, then operated as a division of PSTL & P Company. Service between Bellingham and Mount Vernon began on August 13, 1912. A special train left Bellingham as described in a Stone & Webster journal:

....carrying practically all of the officials of the cities of Mount Vernon, Sedro-Woolley and Bellingham, together with the officials of Whatcom and Skagit Counties, the members of various commercial organizations, and a large representation from an employees' social and cultural activities association called the Stone & Webster Club of Washington.

The completed line ran from the Pike Building at State and Holly in Bellingham, to Burlington, and on to a terminus in Mount Vernon. A branch line ran from Burlington to Sedro-Woolley.

From Andy Loft, Puget Power retiree:

The freight run on the Bellingham and Skagit used to leave at 4:30 in the morning with box cars and flat cars. It would be loaded to the roof with groceries and materials that would go to different stores. We hauled milk cans and everything else. We would unload on the way down and go over to Sedro-Woolley, back to Burlington, down to Mt. Vernon, switch Darigold Company and Pictsweet Company cannery, and then head back north, switching and picking up along the way. Many times we had to cut the train and run in light to beat the so-called "hog law." You couldn't work more than 16 hours, so we had to hurry.

The rail link between Mount Vernon and Everett was never built. There were several reasons for this,

among them the business depression that began in 1912 and continued for several years; World War I and its shortages of materials; lack of investment capital; growing competition from bus companies; the increasing use of automobiles and trucks; and competition from Great Northern Railroad. Further, this would have been a very expensive line to build, requiring crossings of the Stillaguamish and Skykomish Rivers, and building across the extensive marshlands between Everett and Marysville. Instead of rail, Pacific Northwest Traction provided bus service between Everett and Mount Vernon, which required changes in both cities.

Heyday

From 1912 on, the interurban railways consolidated under Stone &

Above: Whatcom County Railway and Light Co. car crossing the Chuckanut Creek Bridge.

Left: A highlight of the Bellingham-Skagit interurban ride was crossing the scenic four-mile trestle along the shore of Samish Bay.

Webster were operated and maintained as divisions of Puget Sound Traction, Light & Power Company. These electric railways were a vital part of the physical, social and economic life of their day. They provided local transportation for commuting workers; shoppers; students commuting to schools and colleges in Bellingham, Seattle and Tacoma; friends and relatives visiting for holidays and special events. Bellingham Bay Electric even had a special car used only for funerals. The electric railways replaced the horse-drawn car in metropolitan areas and the stagecoach for travel between cities.

Electric railways moved milk, vegetables and other farm products quickly to markets. Lumber mills were served by switching cars to the main-line railroads and to port facilities. Most of the industrial growth of the area was influenced by the availability of service from a local electric railway. Many small businesses owed their very existence to the lines.

Passenger fares provided about 80 percent of the revenues, freight about 20 percent. But freight was important: PSE owned a coal mine at Renton that produced 400 to 500 tons daily. Five thousand gallons of milk were handled daily

August 31, 1912: The Pacific Northwest Traction Company's opening day.

Courtesy of CPNS, WWU

Andy Loft

*I*n 1912, the year Puget Sound Traction, Light & Power was consolidated, a Bellingham teenager got his first job cleaning up the shops of the Bellingham-Skagit Interurban electric railway — for fifty cents a day. When he retired 51 years later, Andy Loft had logged more time with Puget Power than any employee before or since.

From 1912 to 1963, Loft served the company as freight brakeman, interurban conductor, sales representative and Mount Vernon Local Manager. A loyal and beloved employee, he is renowned for a lifetime of community service, through churches, Chambers of Commerce, the Red Cross, the Elks Club and Rotary International.

But he's most fondly remembered as a walking encyclopedia of the golden days of the interurban. He spent much of his later years at Puget Power, as well as his retirement, presenting a slide-talk on the electric

railway systems, and what it was like to be one of the people who made them run in their heyday.

Can't tell a trolley from a cable car?

Railroad buffs value precise terminology. What do we mean by streetcar, trolley, cable car and railway?

A **streetcar** is a large coach or car for public transportation that follows a regular route along public roads, usually on steel rails. Early streetcars were pulled by horses. When electricity came in, streetcar systems were of two types: trolley and cable.

A **trolley** is a carriage or basket that runs suspended with wheels on an overhead track or cable. A ski lift is a trolley system. In street transportation, a trolley is an apparatus for collecting electric current from an overhead wire and transmitting it to a motor of a streetcar.

In contrast to the trolleys, powered by overhead lines, a **cable car** is pulled by a continuously moving underground cable in a slot between the rails, to which the car is attached by a grip that can be released to halt the car. Cable cars were used on steep hills or up canyon walls.

A **railway** is a road laid with parallel steel rails upon which cars carrying passengers or freight are drawn by locomotives. Seattle's first railway was horse-drawn (1884). The earliest railway locomotives were

steam-powered; today's use diesel-fuel. But during the short heyday of electric transportation, trains were powered either by overhead trolleys or by an electrified "third rail" on the ground.

Yesler Way cable car on Seattle's Leschi Bridge, 1910. Note the slot between the rails, through which the car was connected to a moving underground cable.

Photo by Asahel Curtis
Courtesy of the U of W Libraries

P.S.E.'s Seattle-Tacoma interurban operated from 1900 to 1928. This Brill car, crossing the Renton Valley, could operate from overhead power lines or from an electrified third rail as shown here.

Photo by Asahel Curtis
Courtesy of the Washington State Historical Society

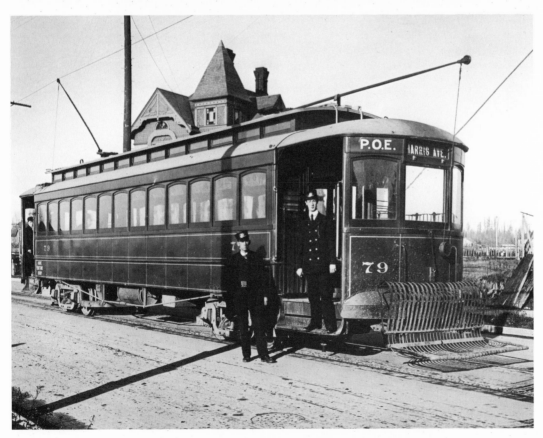

Pay-on-entry (P.O.E.) was a new policy when this trolley car operated (by overhead power lines) on the Harris Avenue run, Bellingham, circa 1925. In the doorway: Andy Loft [see page 31].

Courtesy of the U of W Libraries

in King County. PSE had 23 spur lines into wood, coal and industrial plants in Tacoma. For years the freight business was handled by the "Spud Local." It usually carried three cars of merchandise, two cars of fresh meat, several cars of local freight and some company freight. Farm produce was hauled at night.

One of the most powerful reasons for building these systems was the interest of real estate developers and landowners in providing access to new areas where homes could be built. These promoters were involved in all the early ventures, and accomplished most of their goals.

Decline and Fall

The Puget Sound Electric Railway enjoyed good business before the coming of the automobile and the truck. The building of hard surfaced roads by the state brought thousands of autos, jitney buses, motor coaches and trucks. At no time was non-stop-passenger-express business of greatest importance; there were always more local passengers, and this made for slower service. Bus and truck routes were more flexible and could be changed daily. After World War I the through-railroads competed for passenger service by cutting fares, and during the 1920s competed vigorously for freight traffic. 1919 was PSE's best year ever, financially — almost three million passengers were carried. Then the decline began.

The Puget Sound Traction, Light & Power Company sold the Seattle street railway system to the City of Seattle in 1919 [more in Chapter 6]. But it was a losing battle on other holdings. PSE lost heavily during the twenties, with the parent company having to subsidize operations. Early

Riding the electric rails: An experience that's gone forever.

Courtesy of the U of W Libraries

in 1928 PSE filed for bankruptcy and notified the Public Service Commission of its intent to cease operations. The state appointed a receiver who immediately announced that he intended to keep the cars rolling. The receiver attempted to rehabilitate the earning power of the interurban, but admitted defeat in late 1928.

The report of the receiver of the Puget Sound Electric Railway showed a book value of $5,777,365 and total liabilities of $9,017,615.

In April 1925 Pacific Northwest Traction agreed with Pacific Stages of Vancouver, British Columbia, to provide through-bus service between Seattle and Bellingham, with connections at Bellingham for Vancouver. This put the company in direct competition with its own

Above: The coming of paved streets heralded the ascendancy of the bus, truck and automobile, and the decline of rail transport.

Courtesy of the U of W Libraries

Left: William H. "Bill" Somers was a manager with Pacific Northwest Traction and Puget Sound Electric Railway during the heyday of electric rail transport. As an executive with North Coast Transportation Company, he presided over the transition from electric railway lines to motor bus operations.

interurbans. The separate Interurban Motor Company name was dropped, and a bus division was created to serve as an equal partner with the railroad division. Equipment was spruced up. The new 27-passenger motor stages were painted with a cream top, a Boston grey bottom, and a four-inch red stripe around the middle. In May 1926 a new agreement gave both Pacific Northwest Traction and Pacific Stages the right to operate one round-trip daily between Seattle and Vancouver, without a bus change in Bellingham.

Encouraged by the success of the through-service between Seattle and Vancouver, PNT introduced a new schedule in January 1927 that would result in the final collapse of railway operations on the Pacific Northwest Traction line. This schedule provided hourly service between Seattle and Bellingham, seven trips entirely by motor coach and seven trips by a combination of motor coach and interurban connection. Motor coaches soon took all of the business, since no one wanted to bother with a change in Mount Vernon.

Because of declining revenues, maintenance was neglected and the interurban right-of-way began to deteriorate. There were derailments

Above: At 26, Walter Shannon was the youngest — and the last — motorman hired to work on the Seattle-Everett interurban. He made the transition to North Coast bus driver in 1938, when this photo was taken, and continued to drive buses until 1955.

Right: The new and the old: a motor bus in front of the Everett Interurban Terminal.

at Inspiration Point and Rocky Point; and in October 1928, the Skagit River bridge was condemned as unsafe. The bridge was rebuilt, but the stock market crash in October 1929 hurt Stone & Webster's plans for continuing service. The rail line was officially abandoned in June 1930. The last streetcar to operate on the Bellingham street line ran on December 31, 1938.

Despite efforts of civic organizations to save the big, green cars, the last interurban between Seattle and Everett rolled on February 20, 1939. The day of the bus had dawned.

All of the motor coach business became a part of North Coast Transportation Company. This was now an important regional carrier, offering passenger service from

Vancouver, British Columbia to Portland, Oregon and points along the way. North Coast was sold to Greyhound Corporation in 1947, which ended company participation in the transportation of passengers.

10 p.m., February 20, 1939: The Last Interurban Ride. One of the motormen on the last day of service was Arthur Amundson, Walter Shannon's father-in-law.

The coming of the family car.

Right: The derailment of Car #75 at Rocky Point, on the Samish Bay trestle, September, 1928 , brought the deteriorating state of the interurban lines to public attention. As the rail lines' fortunes declined, it became less possible to maintain lines and equipment in safe condition, and so even harder to compete with new rubber-wheeled motor vehicles.

This rise and fall of the interurban is not unique to the Puget Sound region. Henry Ford introduced the Model T just when street railways and interurban lines were forming extremely important systems all over the United States. Few business leaders and city officials could forsee that the motor car would easily win the competition for passenger traffic. Local fares were usually five cents as compared with the $500 price of a Model T. There was no vision of every family owning a car. Wall Street investors believed in the interurbans and backed them, but it proved to be a bad decision.

In a review of the interurbans, George W. Hilton and John F. Due have observed:

> *Few industries have arisen so rapidly or declined so quickly, and no industry of its size had a worse financial record. The interurbans were a rare example of an industry that never enjoyed a period of prolonged prosperity.*[1]

[1] *The Electric Railway Era, 1890-1930,* Daniel E. Turbeville, 1978.

Courtesy of the Museum
of History & Industry

CHAPTER 5

Puget Power comes of age

Electric railways were still young, and far from decline, when Jacob Furth became president of Seattle Electric Company in 1900. In Furth, Charles Stone had found a man of eminent scope and capability. Furth's first order of business was to consolidate the operations of the ten principal Seattle utility and street car businesses included in the merger that had created Seattle Electric Company. These included:

- Madison Street Cable Railway Co.
- Burke Block Light Plant
- Consumers Electric Co.
- Seattle Steam Heat & Power Co.
- Union Trunk Line
- Union Electric Co.
- Third Street & Suburban Railway Co.
- First Avenue (Cable) Railway Co.
- Seattle Traction Co.
- Grant Street Electric Railway Co.

[See the accompanying chart, *The Puget Power Family Tree,* page 46-47.]

That accomplished, Furth hardly paused to catch his breath. In 1901 Seattle Electric acquired the West Street & North End Railway Company and the Seattle Railway Company. In 1902 the Seattle Central Railway Company was acquired. Arcade Electric Company and the Electric Department of Seattle Gas & Electric Company were added in 1903. The West Seattle Municipal Street Railway Company was acquired in 1907. In 1902 Furth aided in organizing—and became president of — the Puget Sound Electric Railway, controlling

Charles Baker's Seattle Cataract Company administered sales of Snoqualmie power from this building, shown here under construction.

the lines between Seattle and Tacoma and the Tacoma streetcar system. He accomplished all of this formidable activity as a part-time endeavor, while continuing as president of Seattle National Bank and director of several other businesses.

Meanwhile Stone & Webster people were busy acquiring and consolidating other fledgling utility and street railway operations in western Washington. Four of these were later to become part of Puget Power:

Seattle-Tacoma Power Company

In 1897 Charles H. Baker had acquired the water power lands

Snoqualmie

and rights at Snoqualmie Falls. He organized the Snoqualmie Falls Power Company and built the famous plant [described in Chapter 2]. He then organized the Seattle Cataract Company and the Tacoma Cataract Company, which delivered power to their respective cities.

Eyeing the astounding demand for electricity in the early 1900s, Baker now turned his attention toward a site on the White River, on which options had been secured in 1895 by the White River Power Company of

New York. It was available. For a year, October 1902 to October 1903, the Snoqualmie Falls Power Company and the White River Power Company jointly purchased land essential to the site development.

In 1904, after Baker's departure, the three companies — Snoqualmie Falls, Seattle Cataract and Tacoma Cataract — merged as Seattle-Tacoma Power Company. In 1905 this company purchased the plant and assets of Mutual Light and Heat Company in Seattle, and in 1906 it purchased the assets of the White River Power Company. Now it alone controlled the hydro site. The price

Jacob Furth (1840-1914), the first president of Seattle Electric Co., was a grandparent of Puget Power. Furth, born in Bohemia, came to Seattle in 1882. He founded the Puget Sound National Bank and quickly became one of the city's leading citizens, serving on the city council from 1885 to 1891.

was $1,250,000. It had over-extended its finances.

In January 1908, to satisfy a mortgage, the Seattle-Tacoma Power Company quit-claimed and conveyed all lands heretofore held by the White River Power Company to the Pacific Coast Power Company, a subsidiary of the Seattle Electric Company. The consideration was $583,333. A competitor now owned the site and proceeded to build the White River Hydro Project.

Pacific Coast Power Company

Tacoma Industrial Company was organized in 1902 and acquired from S. L. Shuffleton certain lands, water

White River

rights and buildings located on White River. In 1903 it acquired Puyallup Electric Company, which had plants and distribution systems in both Puyallup and Sumner. Pacific Coast Power Company, organized in 1908, took over all property of Tacoma Power Company, and at the site acquired from the Seattle-Tacoma Power Company, it built the White River plant, completed in 1911. This company had been under the management of Stone & Webster since 1902.

Puget Sound Power Company

First incorporated as Pierce County Improvement Company in 1902, this firm changed its name to Puget Sound Power Company in 1903. It was organized by Stone &

A "donkey engine" during the construction of White River plant, 1900.

Webster to build and operate a power plant on the Puyallup River at Electron. Power was to be sold to Seattle Electric Company, Puget Sound Electric Railway, and the

Electron

Tacoma Railway & Power Company, all managed by Stone & Webster. The plant was completed in 1904. Operations of this company were directed by Seattle Electric until 1912.

Whatcom County Railway & Light Company

Incorporated in 1902, this company was a consolidation of two utility companies, Whatcom-Fairhaven Gas Company and Northern Railway & Improvement Company. In 1906 it took over from Columbia Improvement Company the light and power system that had been acquired from Bellingham Bay Improvement Company. This consisted of a franchise to furnish power in the City of Bellingham for 40 years, together with land and riparian rights on the Nooksack River. Whatcom County Railway & Light then completed construction of the York Street steam

42

Nooksack

plant and the Nooksack hydro-electric plant. It was then the owner of practically all of the railway, electric light and power, and gas systems in the City of Bellingham.

Changing the Rules

This maturing process of consolidation brought with it and increasing awareness of problems requiring industry-wide solutions. There was genuine concern about minimum standards for generating, transmission and distribution materials and equipment. Safety had been largely ignored by the small companies whose distribution lines were often bare wires fastened to buildings and trees. There were no uniform requirements for standards of service. Rates were not regulated and often were all the traffic would bear. This led to an unusual number of requests to the Washington State Legislature to pass laws and approve regulations for the industry.

The Railroad Commission of Washington was established in 1905 with limited power to regulate the rates, services and facilities of railroad and express companies. In 1909 its regulatory powers and duties were extended through more comprehensive legislation. In 1911 the name was changed to the Public Service Commission of Washington, which had authority to:

...regulate, in the public interest,

Samuel L. Shuffleton

Courtesy of the
U of W Libraries

*I*n the city of Renton stands Shuffleton Steam Plant — for years an important augmentation of Puget Power's hydro-electric resources, and more recently a stand-by resource in time of unusually high power demand. The plant's name makes it a continuing monument to the memory of Samuel L. Shuffleton, civil engineer par excellance.

Born in 1864 in frontier California, the son of an itinerant printer turned gold prospector turned farmer, Shuffleton practiced civil engineering in Eureka for nearly a decade before coming to Seattle in 1890 to join Stone & Webster. He was later made western manager of Stone & Webster Engineering Corporation. Among the construction projects completed under Shuffleton's management were office buildings for the Seattle Electric Company, Puget Power's Electron and White River hydroelectric projects, and the titanic 120-mile, 25,000-kilowatt trans-Cascade transmission line linking Seattle with Wenatchee.

Shuffleton also managed hydro-electric plant construction projects

throughout the west, including major facilities of Pacific Light and Power and Southern California Edison. He was one of a very few West Coast natives involved in the first shaping of Puget Power, and was praised in a Seattle history book from the '20s as one who "has few rivals in the field of engineering construction" — an observation that holds true even today.

Shuffleton inspecting one of the White River plants.

Photo by Asahel Curtis
Courtesy of the
Washington State
Historical Society

the rates, services, facilities and practices . . . of those engaged in the business of supplying any utility service or commodity to the public for compensation, and related activities, and to prescribe such rules and regulations as may be necessary to carry out its power and duties.

The rules of the game changed overnight. No longer was each electric light company or streetcar line to be regulated by the local political authority that had granted its franchise. Stone & Webster was now confronted with the necessity of dealing with a new state agency on behalf of all of its operating units involved in the generation, transmission, distribution and sale of electric power to the public, and also the operation of several electric street railways. The time had come to consolidate their various holdings to permit greater efficiency, better management, and uniformity in dealing with the Public Service Commission.

Enter Puget Power

Puget Sound Traction, Light & Power Company was first organized in the State of Maine in January 1912. The company was reincorporated, with no change in name or property, in the State of Massachusetts on July 15, 1912, with Jacob Furth as president.

During 1912 this new company acquired all of the assets and assumed all of the liabilties of several companies, principally through an exchange of stock, followed by the liquidation of these companies:

- Seattle-Tacoma Power Co., as of January 1, 1912
- Pacific Coast Power Co., as of January 16, 1912
- Seattle Electric Co., as of April 1, 1912
- Puget Sound Power Co., as of May 1, 1912
- Whatcom County Railway & Light Co., as of September 1, 1912
- Puget Sound Electric Railway
- Pacific Northwest Traction Co.
- Puget Sound International Railway & Power Co. (Everett)

According to company records, no fewer than 57 separate public

The steam generating plant at York Street, Bellingham, in December, 1910.

Courtesy of the U of W Libraries

44

utility companies had preceded Puget Sound Traction, Light & Power Company, the majority of them predecessors of Seattle Electric Company. With these companies came four hydroelectric plants at Snoqualmie Falls, White River, Electron and Nooksack; and steam generating plants at Georgetown and Post Street in Seattle and at York Street in Bellingham. There were also light and power distribution systems in Seattle, gas properties in Bellingham and coal mines near Renton.

The first annual report of Puget Sound Traction, Light & Power Company was issued January 1, 1913 at Boston, Massachusetts. It gave a summary of the consolidation of properties that had taken place in

1912. Here are a few items extracted from that report:

Total revenue	$8,313.847
Operating expenses and taxes	$4,772,298
Operating income	$3,541,549
For interest and sinking funds	$1,976,250
Net earnings	$1,565,299
Dividends paid (including subsidiaries)	$1,277,787
Balance carried forward	$287,511
Number of power and light customers	29,148
Number of employees (all companies)	3,409
Interurban, street railways, miles of track	472.9
Street cars owned	599 passenger, 192 freight and mail
Interurban cars owned	45 passenger, 205 freight and mail
Total number of passengers carried	136,161,261

For most customers, the incorporation of the Puget Sound Traction, Light & Power Company had little meaning at the moment. As a Massachusetts corporation, it would hold all meetings of directors or stockholders in far-off Boston, "where the important decisions were already being made anyway." This latest reorganization was just part of another corporate day's work.

Left: Seattle's Post Street steam plant.

Courtesy of the U of W Libraries

Below: A Puget Power service truck dating from the second decade of the 20th century.

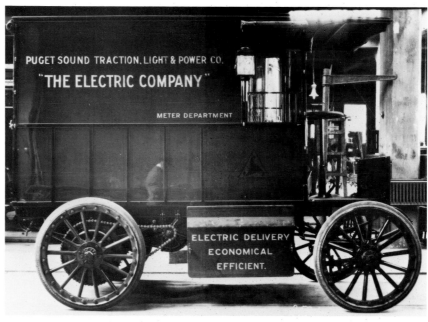

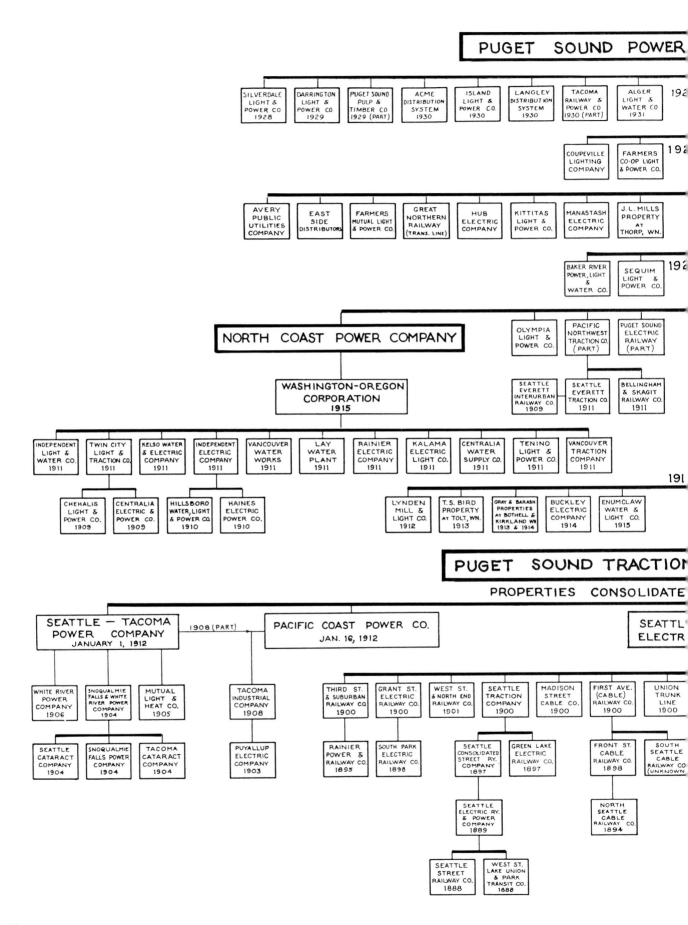

PUGET SOUND POWER

| | | | | | | | | 192 |

| SILVERDALE LIGHT & POWER CO 1928 | DARRINGTON LIGHT & POWER CO. 1929 | PUGET SOUND PULP & TIMBER CO. 1929 (PART) | ACME DISTRIBUTION SYSTEM 1930 | ISLAND LIGHT & POWER CO. 1930 | LANGLEY DISTRIBUTION SYSTEM 1930 | TACOMA RAILWAY & POWER CO 1930 (PART) | ALGER LIGHT & WATER CO 1931 |

192

| COUPEVILLE LIGHTING COMPANY | FARMERS CO-OP LIGHT & POWER CO. |

| AVERY PUBLIC UTILITIES COMPANY | EAST SIDE DISTRIBUTORS | FARMERS MUTUAL LIGHT & POWER CO. | GREAT NORTHERN RAILWAY (TRANS. LINE) | HUB ELECTRIC COMPANY | KITTITAS LIGHT & POWER CO. | MANASTASH ELECTRIC COMPANY | J. L. MILLS PROPERTY AT THORP, WN. |

192

| BAKER RIVER POWER, LIGHT & WATER CO. | SEQUIM LIGHT & POWER CO. |

NORTH COAST POWER COMPANY

| OLYMPIA LIGHT & POWER CO. | PACIFIC NORTHWEST TRACTION CO. (PART) | PUGET SOUND ELECTRIC RAILWAY (PART) |

WASHINGTON-OREGON CORPORATION 1915

| SEATTLE EVERETT INTERURBAN RAILWAY CO. 1909 | SEATTLE EVERETT TRACTION CO. 1911 | BELLINGHAM & SKAGIT RAILWAY CO. 1911 |

| INDEPENDENT LIGHT & WATER CO. 1911 | TWIN CITY LIGHT & TRACTION CO. 1911 | KELSO WATER & ELECTRIC COMPANY 1911 | INDEPENDENT ELECTRIC COMPANY 1911 | VANCOUVER WATER WORKS 1911 | LAY WATER PLANT 1911 | RAINIER ELECTRIC COMPANY 1911 | KALAMA ELECTRIC LIGHT CO. 1911 | CENTRALIA WATER SUPPLY CO. 1911 | TENINO LIGHT & POWER CO. 1911 | VANCOUVER TRACTION COMPANY 1911 |

191

| CHEHALIS LIGHT & POWER CO. 1909 | CENTRALIA ELECTRIC & POWER CO. 1909 | HILLSBORO WATER, LIGHT & POWER CO. 1910 | HAINES ELECTRIC POWER CO. 1910 | | LYNDEN MILL & LIGHT CO. 1912 | T. S. BIRD PROPERTY AT TOLT, WN. 1913 | GRAY & BARASH PROPERTIES AT BOTHELL & KIRKLAND WN. 1913 & 1914 | BUCKLEY ELECTRIC COMPANY 1914 | ENUMCLAW WATER & LIGHT CO. 1915 |

PUGET SOUND TRACTION

PROPERTIES CONSOLIDATE

| SEATTLE – TACOMA POWER COMPANY JANUARY 1, 1912 | 1908 (PART) | PACIFIC COAST POWER CO. JAN. 16, 1912 | | SEATTL ELECTR |

| WHITE RIVER POWER COMPANY 1906 | SNOQUALMIE FALLS & WHITE RIVER POWER COMPANY 1904 | MUTUAL LIGHT & HEAT CO. 1905 | | TACOMA INDUSTRIAL COMPANY 1908 | | THIRD ST. & SUBURBAN RAILWAY CO. 1900 | GRANT ST. ELECTRIC RAILWAY CO. 1900 | WEST ST. & NORTH END RAILWAY CO. 1901 | SEATTLE TRACTION COMPANY 1900 | MADISON STREET CABLE CO. 1900 | FIRST AVE. (CABLE) RAILWAY CO. 1900 | UNION TRUNK LINE 1900 |

| SEATTLE CATARACT COMPANY 1904 | SNOQUALMIE FALLS POWER COMPANY 1904 | TACOMA CATARACT COMPANY 1904 | | PUYALLUP ELECTRIC COMPANY 1903 | | RAINIER POWER & RAILWAY CO. 1895 | SOUTH PARK ELECTRIC RAILWAY CO. 1898 | SEATTLE CONSOLIDATED STREET RY. COMPANY 1897 | GREEN LAKE ELECTRIC RAILWAY CO. 1897 | | FRONT ST. CABLE RAILWAY CO. 1898 | SOUTH SEATTLE CABLE RAILWAY CO. (UNKNOWN) |

| | | SEATTLE ELECTRIC RY. & POWER COMPANY 1889 | | NORTH SEATTLE CABLE RAILWAY CO. 1894 |

| SEATTLE STREET RAILWAY CO. 1888 | WEST ST. LAKE UNION & PARK TRANSIT CO. 1888 |

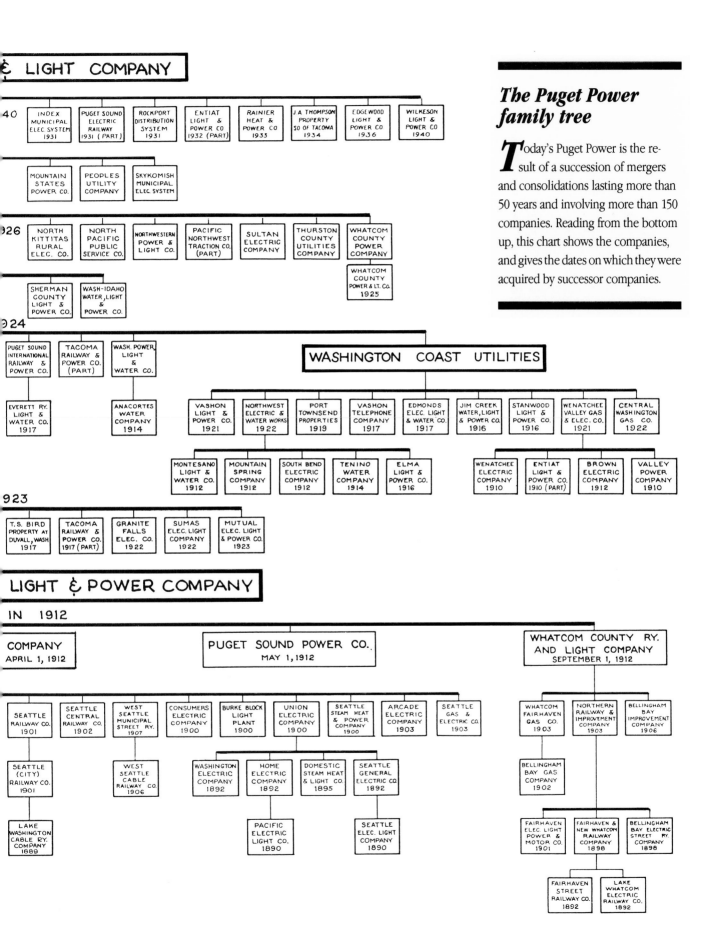

Ε LIGHT COMPANY

40
- INDEX MUNICIPAL ELEC. SYSTEM 1931
- PUGET SOUND ELECTRIC RAILWAY 1931 (PART)
- ROCKPORT DISTRIBUTION SYSTEM 1931
- ENTIAT LIGHT & POWER CO. 1932 (PART)
- RAINIER HEAT & POWER CO. 1933
- J.A. THOMPSON PROPERTY SO OF TACOMA 1934
- EDGEWOOD LIGHT & POWER CO. 1936
- WILKESON LIGHT & POWER CO. 1940

- MOUNTAIN STATES POWER CO.
- PEOPLES UTILITY COMPANY
- SKYKOMISH MUNICIPAL ELEC. SYSTEM

26
- NORTH KITTITAS RURAL ELEC. CO.
- NORTH PACIFIC PUBLIC SERVICE CO.
- NORTHWESTERN POWER & LIGHT CO.
- PACIFIC NORTHWEST TRACTION CO. (PART)
- SULTAN ELECTRIC COMPANY
- THURSTON COUNTY UTILITIES COMPANY
- WHATCOM COUNTY POWER COMPANY
  - WHATCOM COUNTY POWER & LT. CO. 1925

- SHERMAN COUNTY LIGHT & POWER CO.
- WASH-IDAHO WATER, LIGHT & POWER CO.

24
- PUGET SOUND INTERNATIONAL RAILWAY & POWER CO.
- TACOMA RAILWAY & POWER CO. (PART)
- WASH. POWER LIGHT & WATER CO.
  - EVERETT RY. LIGHT & WATER CO. 1917
  - ANACORTES WATER COMPANY 1914

WASHINGTON COAST UTILITIES
- VASHON LIGHT & POWER CO. 1921
- NORTHWEST ELECTRIC & WATER WORKS 1922
- PORT TOWNSEND PROPERTIES 1919
- VASHON TELEPHONE COMPANY 1917
- EDMONDS ELEC. LIGHT & WATER CO. 1917
- JIM CREEK WATER, LIGHT & POWER CO. 1916
- STANWOOD LIGHT & POWER CO. 1916
- WENATCHEE VALLEY GAS & ELEC. CO. 1921
- CENTRAL WASHINGTON GAS CO. 1922

  - MONTESANO LIGHT & WATER CO. 1912
  - MOUNTAIN SPRING COMPANY 1912
  - SOUTH BEND ELECTRIC COMPANY 1912
  - TENINO WATER COMPANY 1914
  - ELMA LIGHT & POWER CO. 1916
  - WENATCHEE ELECTRIC COMPANY 1910
  - ENTIAT LIGHT & POWER CO. 1910 (PART)
  - BROWN ELECTRIC COMPANY 1912
  - VALLEY POWER COMPANY 1910

23
- T.S. BIRD PROPERTY AT DUVALL, WASH 1917
- TACOMA RAILWAY & POWER CO. 1917 (PART)
- GRANITE FALLS ELEC. CO. 1922
- SUMAS ELEC. LIGHT COMPANY 1922
- MUTUAL ELEC. LIGHT & POWER CO. 1923

LIGHT Ε POWER COMPANY

IN 1912

- COMPANY APRIL 1, 1912
- PUGET SOUND POWER CO. MAY 1, 1912
- WHATCOM COUNTY RY. AND LIGHT COMPANY SEPTEMBER 1, 1912

- SEATTLE RAILWAY CO. 1901
  - SEATTLE (CITY) RAILWAY CO. 1901
    - LAKE WASHINGTON CABLE RY. COMPANY 1889
- SEATTLE CENTRAL RAILWAY CO. 1902
- WEST SEATTLE MUNICIPAL STREET RY. 1907
  - WEST SEATTLE CABLE RAILWAY CO. 1906
- CONSUMERS ELECTRIC COMPANY 1900
- BURKE BLOCK LIGHT PLANT 1900
  - WASHINGTON ELECTRIC COMPANY 1892
  - HOME ELECTRIC COMPANY 1892
    - PACIFIC ELECTRIC LIGHT CO. 1890
- UNION ELECTRIC COMPANY 1900
  - DOMESTIC STEAM HEAT & LIGHT CO. 1895
- SEATTLE STEAM HEAT & POWER COMPANY 1900
  - SEATTLE GENERAL ELECTRIC CO. 1892
    - SEATTLE ELEC. LIGHT COMPANY 1890
- ARCADE ELECTRIC COMPANY 1903
- SEATTLE GAS & ELECTRIC CO. 1903

- WHATCOM FAIRHAVEN GAS CO. 1903
  - BELLINGHAM BAY GAS COMPANY 1902
    - FAIRHAVEN ELEC. LIGHT POWER & MOTOR CO. 1901
- NORTHERN RAILWAY & IMPROVEMENT COMPANY 1903
  - FAIRHAVEN & NEW WHATCOM RAILWAY COMPANY 1898
    - FAIRHAVEN STREET RAILWAY CO. 1892
    - LAKE WHATCOM ELECTRIC RAILWAY CO. 1892
- BELLINGHAM BAY IMPROVEMENT COMPANY 1906
  - BELLINGHAM BAY ELECTRIC STREET RY. COMPANY 1898

The Puget Power family tree

*T*oday's Puget Power is the result of a succession of mergers and consolidations lasting more than 50 years and involving more than 150 companies. Reading from the bottom up, this chart shows the companies, and gives the dates on which they were acquired by successor companies.

But for Jacob Furth this was an important point of progress — a moment of great satisfaction. From that day in 1900 when he became president of Seattle Electric Company, he had set his sights on an area-wide system. To a great extent it was his leadership, his grasp of the local (social, economic, and political) situation that had made it possible to reach his goal. Even the formation of Seattle City Light in 1904, the opening thrust of a nearly 50-year battle with public power advocates, did not slow Furth's efforts toward ever more improved service. The first year's operating figures indicated that the expanded company was financially sound. In 1913 Furth could justifiably say that Puget Power had "come of age."

In succeeding years, through 1940, there was a major effort to acquire more utility properties in western and central Washington. These companies operated steam and hydro-electric generating plants and electric street railway systems, and provided customers with power, light, gas, water and telephone service. There seems to have been an unwritten policy that the company would stick to electric railway systems,

power and light, and would sell off water, gas and telephone companies as quickly as possible. The total number of companies acquired, including predecessor companies is more than 150. Properties were located in nineteen counties: Chelan, Clallam, Clark, Cowlitz, Douglas, Grays Harbor, Island, Jefferson, King, Kitsap, Kittitas, Lewis, Mason, Pacific, Pierce, Skagit, Snohomish, Thurston and Whatcom.

Jacob Furth would not live to see the full development of his "area-wide system." On June 2, 1914,

following a recurring stomach ailment for which he sought treatment in California, he died. The record shows that he was one of the most highly respected business leaders in western Washington. His leadership was recognized in the fields of banking, metal industries and real estate development, as well as electric utilities and street railways. But the position he most frequently listed first among his accomplishments was serving as president of Puget Sound Traction, Light & Power Company.

PUGET SOUND POWER & LIGHT COMPANY

Puget Power's 19-county service area in 1940.
[Compare with today's nine-county service
area, see map page 166.]

WHATCOM

SKAGIT

ISLAND

CLALLAM

JEFFERSON

SNOHOMISH

CHELAN

KITSAP

DOUGLAS

MASON

KING

GRAYS
HARBOR

KITTITAS

GRANT

PIERCE

THURSTON

PACIFIC

LEWIS

COWLITZ

W A S H I N G T O N

CLARK

☐ Puget Power Service Area, 1940

O R E G O N

Alaska Yukon Expo

On June 1, 1909, President William Howard Taft entered the East Room of the White House, seated himself at a table and at precisely noon pressed a telegraph key that had a contact point made of a gold nugget from the Klondike.

The electric impulse from the contact instantly crossed the continent to Seattle, where a stand draped with bunting stood near the entrance to the world's fair on the University of Washington campus. The impulse triggered a switch that lit electric lights atop a telegraph pole. A cheer arose as the Alaska-Yukon-Pacific Exposition gates swung open. The objective of the Expo was to tell the world of the value of Alaska and to illustrate that Seattle was the gateway not only to the far north but to the Pacific.

The AYP entertained 3,740,551 visitors and earned a surplus of $63,000, which was donated to charity. On the evening of October 16, Exposition President J.E. Chilberg declared, "The fair is ended," and turned a switch that caused the 150,000 electric light globes festooning the fair buildings to go dark. The campus was returned to the University.

CHAPTER 6

Sell, build,
sell, build

When Puget Sound Traction, Light and Power Company was organized in 1912, power was supplied by seven major plants: hydroelectric plants at Snoqualmie Falls, White River, Electron and Nooksack; and the steam plants at Georgetown and Post Street in Seattle and York Street in Bellingham. One of the first achievements of the new company was to link these plants with 55,000-volt transmission lines. This took care of any local shortages and improved system reliability.

Between 1912 and 1920, eight more utility companies in the Puget Sound region were purchased and integrated into this system. From 1920 to 1940 the company pursued an active program of acquiring utility companies in central and western Washington; more than 50 were added, many with their own generating facilities.

In this period of unparalleled growth, the demand for electric power was almost insatiable. New residential, commercial and industrial customers were added almost as fast as lines could be built and service connections made. Street railways and interurbans took large blocks of power. Farm electrification was emphasized, and in 1913 near Lynden, Puget Power constructed

Above: Puget Power linemen working near Seattle's waterfront during the 1920s.

Right: Sales managers at a 1924 meeting. From left, front row: R.W. Lindley, Bellingham; R.W. Clark, Seattle; H.J. Gille, General Sales Manager, Seattle; R.C. Saunders, Tacoma; H.S. Atwood, Everett. Back row: L.M. Shreve, Wenatchee; C.E. Day, Chehalis; Jack Murton, Hillsboro, Oregon; E.A. Batwell, Seattle; L.R. Grant, Seattle.

Georgetown steam plant

John Scott

John C. Scott (1926 to 1939) was Director of Farm Electrification. He established the Research Laboratory at Puyallup where many applications of electricity to farming were developed. These included soil sterilization, electric soil heating cables, greenhouse heating, electric brooding, stump burners and so on. "Happy" Scott was the favorite of farm groups for his programs, which usually started with singing. In recognition of his work, Scott was awarded the Thomas W. Martin Rural Electrification Award for 1934.

A dairy farm worker of the late '20s uses an electric milk stirrer and bottling machine.

Background: an electric milk cooler.

Photo by Asahel Curtis Courtesy of the Washington State Historical Society

what is believed to be the first power line in the United States built specifically to serve farm customers. The Lynden egg and poultry industry flourished as a result. By 1920 Puget Power had electrified about half the farms in its territory; by 1928 the figure was up to sixty-three percent, compared with only three percent nationally.

Company employees contributed a remarkable number of innovative designs for electric products for use on farms including the electric brooder, egg buffer and candler, stump burner, milk cooler, bulb counter, logging fire fan, insect trap, incinerator, sprayer, soil sterilizer, hotbed heating cable, yard lights, irrigation pumps, and greenhouses with heaters, fans and lighting. In 1925 at Puyallup, the company established a Farm Power Laboratory, unique in the nation, to demonstrate and promote the labor-saving uses of electric power on the farm.

In its own shops the company developed the first automatic, insulated water heater, known as the "20-year Monel" (for the rust-resistant material used for the shell). The water heaters were initially manufactured by Wesix Company. An electric range designed and built to company specifications became known as the "Trail Blazer." Refrigerators were tested, and the company selected the General Electric monitor-top as the best. These three appliances formed the basis for marketing the early all-electric home in competition with wood, coal and oil.

In those days, power supply capacity and power use were never in balance for long. When a surplus existed, efforts to "sell" were increased, and customers were shown new ways to use electricity. When power use began to catch up to power supply, sales efforts would be cut back or eliminated. The company would then increase the power supply by expanding existing plants or building new ones. And since new larger-capacity generating units produced power at successively lower costs, the interests of both customers and investors were well served.

More Plants

Stone & Webster believed in long-range planning and were quite thorough in applying it to power supply. From 1912 on, the company annually projected growth and power use 10 years into the future. At the appropriate times, steps were taken to bring additional power supply into the system.

In 1914 the White River plant,

Clere Alger

Clere Alger joined Puget Power in 1922 as a meter tester, and retired in 1945 as Assistant Engineer. Alger was responsible for a series of tests involving Puget Power's "20-year guaranteed Monel Water Heater," which, with the Hotpoint Trailblazer Range, was the backbone of the "all-electric" rate. Subsequently, he was made responsible for the engineering of meters and services, load analysis, and (with John Hewitt, State Electrical Inspector) developing and interpreting state electrical codes. Alger was active in the Seattle Section of American Institute of Electrical Engineers, Chairman of Meter and Service Committee of Northwest Electric Light and Power Association, and President of the Northwest Section of International Association of Electrical Inspectors.

The Monel water heater is featured in 1939 window display in Puget Power's Ballard office.

originally put into service in 1911, was expanded from 20,000 KW to 65,000 KW—the only major generation project of the decade. In 1914 normal sales efforts were eliminated due to wartime restrictions and increased power needs of the shipyards and other war-related industries. In 1919 the sale of the Seattle electric street railway system to the City of Seattle released a block of power for other uses. In 1922 a 120-mile, 110,000 volt transmission line was built across the Cascade Mountains (another first for the company), linking the Beverly Park switching station in Everett with and Wenatchee.

The Baker River plant came on line in 1925 with an initial capacity of 40,000 KW. Of course new generating plants required additional interconnections to reach customer distribution lines. Another "first" for Puget Power was the installation in 1926 of the cross-Sound submarine cable from Richmond Beach, north of Seattle, to President's Point, south of Kingston on the Kitsap Penninsula. Shuffleton steam plant was built in 1929, producing 40,000 KW just in time to save the region from a power shortage caused by a low-water year. Shuffleton was expanded by another 40,000 KW in 1930.

Baker River

Below: Stone & Webster workers stringing high-tension cable across Stevens Pass, May, 1927, to power Great Northern Railway electric locomotives through the Cascade Tunnel.

The most ambitious generating project up to that time was undertaken when Rock Island Dam on the Columbia River was started in 1928 by Stone & Webster. This was a truly bold feat of engineering and construction — the first time the mighty Columbia River had been dammed to serve man. When the first four generating units were brought on line in 1933 with 80,000 KW, this block of power, added at the depths of the Great Depression, sparked the greatest sales effort in the company's history.

Below: Rock Island Dam — the first to harness the energy of the Columbia River — under construction in September 1930.

Right: Inspecting the downstream side of Rock Island power house, December 19, 1930: (from left) W.D. Shannon, Stone & Webster general superintendent for the project; Leslie R. Coffin, Puget Power's Central District Manager; R.E. McGrew, construction superintendent.

Leslie R. Coffin

When the Whatcom County Railway and Electric Light Company became part of Puget Sound Traction, Light & Power Co., its manager, Leslie R. Coffin, came with it.

A member of the Stone & Webster organization since his graduation with honors from Harvard in 1906, Coffin had come to Bellingham as a district manager in 1910. It was said that he was the only manager ever to own a Ford — a remark that said volumes in the second decade of the century.

With the formation of Puget Sound Traction, Light & Power in 1912, Coffin became Northern District Manager — in effect, the company's first Northern District Director — a position he held until the United States entered the World War in 1917. He was asked by Stone & Webster to oversee construction at its Hog Island shipyard in Pennyslvania. This was followed by a series of construction management positions in California, and then by a stint of self-employment.

But Puget Power had not seen the last of Leslie Coffin. Indeed, his greatest contribution lay ahead. In 1927 he rejoined the company as Eastern District Manager, headquartered in Wenatchee. There, with a vision comparable to that of Charles Baker three decades earlier, he committed himself to realizing a dream: a mighty hydroelectric dam on the then-untamed Columbia River.

He fixed on Rock Island, 13 miles south of Wenatchee, as the perfect site; and through his tireless efforts, the first dam to span the Columbia became a reality. Rock Island Dam began construction in 1928 and came on line in 1933. By that time, Coffin had moved again: to Seattle, where, in 1931, he became Central District Manager under the company's new president, Frank McLaughlin. He held that post until his death in 1940.

Visionary engineer, tireless community organizer, and an accomplished musician, Coffin is remembered for his precision and judgment. He is said, in fact, to have made only one mistake in his career: He once beat Frank McLaughlin at golf.

As the golden era of the 1920s drew to a close, Puget Power's fortunes began to tarnish. The turn was signaled most clearly in the sudden change in fortune of the company president.

Following the death of Jacob Furth in 1914, Alton William Leonard was named President of Puget Sound Traction, Light and Power Company. His preparation for that responsible assignment had seemed solid indeed.

Born in Monmouth, Maine, April 6, 1873, Leonard completed basic education in the schools of Boston and Brockton, Massachusetts. He started work as a bookkeeper and progressed rapidly. After six years he was made assistant treasurer of the Edison Electric Illuminating Company of Brockton, a Stone & Webster-managed corporation. He had thus been identified as a young man of potential in the Stone & Webster "farm team" training system. There followed promotions: in 1901 to Superintendent of the Houghton County (Michigan) Electric Light Company, in 1905 to Vice President of the Minneapolis General Electric Company, and in 1912 to Vice President and general manager of the Puget Sound Traction, Light and Power Company.

Leonard is remembered as a kindly-mannered, and hard-working leader of the company, proud-to-bursting of the growth achieved by both continued consolidation of smaller companies into Puget Power and the ever-widening public acceptance of the company's service at continually decreasing rates. Under his administration, the company's service territory increased to its high-water mark of 19 western and central Washington counties. Leonard was a gregarious fellow — today we would say a "people person" — and his management style reflected that. He was an active member of one yacht club, seven golf clubs, four fraternal lodges, several hunting clubs and

A.W. Leonard
Courtesy of the Washington State Historical Society

numerous community service organizations. Reflecting the grand style expected (or accepted) of major business leaders of the day, he acquired the 96-foot yacht *Electra*, on which he relished entertaining other community leaders, politicians, and Stone & Webster bigwigs from Boston. Leonard believed strongly that the interests of both his customers and his stockholders required that he be prominent in all business and political affairs of the state and the region served. That he succeeded in doing it his way is indicated by an inscription in the 1929 edition of the Seattle "Kind Words Club" yearbook, that he "owns City Hall and most of the legislature — body, boots and breeches." To whatever extent true,

this would ultimately become more of a cross to bear than a badge of accomplishment.

Measured by the company's contributions to the business and social welfare of the region served, the seventeen years of Leonard's administration were a time of great accomplishment: electricity customers served, up from 34,322 to 156,135; average electricity rates down from 8.7 cents to 3.4 cents per kilowatt-hour; annual net earnings (all operations) up from $1.5 to $4.5 million; and a steady stream of new labor-saving applications for electricity, many invented by company employees to meet the special needs of Washington state businesses.

From the standpoint of his personal career, however, it was a period during which Leonard acquired a growing load of very heavy "baggage." From the moment

he was named president in 1914, Leonard's New England origins, combined with the fact that Stone & Webster (acting for mainly eastern stockholders) was the source of his election, were seized on by the local press as evidence that he was only the agent of "Boston big money power trusters." Columnists and political candidates seemed to revel in competition to see who could couch these labels in the most blistering terms. Only Seattle Times reporter C.T. Conover noted that the eastern capitalists Leonard represented were, in fact, several thousand individual investors with a stake in and around Seattle, and that Stone & Webster was the source of more investment in the growth and improvement of the area than any other business up to that time.

The largest detriment to Leonard's career resulted from the public

Above: Leonard's beloved Electra, as refurbished in 1981, more than 50 years old.

Right: Puget Power promotes the move toward local ownership, a reaction to criticism of East Coast interests during the Leonard years.

reaction to the great 1919 traction transaction — the deal by which the City of Seattle acquired the streetcar

system from Puget Sound Traction, Light & Power Company. The "nickel fare" had been in place since the horse-car days and had become a key part of the culture and expectations of Seattle citizens. When in the midst of World War I the company advised the city that an increased fare was necessary to meet costs (such as the growing expense of repairing that portion of street paving occupied by tracks), an uproar was created focusing once again on those "avaricious Eastern bloodsuckers." The public became convinced that by eliminating "those profiteers" (a wartime term of disapproval) the nickel fare could be preserved. Leonard knew better, but decided the best course was to sell out. Based on an independent appraisal value of $16 million, he negotiated with Mayor Ole Hanson a sale at $15 million, to be paid in the form of an issue of revenue bonds. When the city fathers later learned

that, indeed, the system could not be profitable on the nickel fare, Leonard was accused of seducing Ole Hanson into paying too much for the system. Even after a forced renegotiation of the price down to $10 million, Seattle subsequently defaulted on the payment of portions of both principal and interest. Even more devastating to the company was the residue of ill feeling that would fuel other crises for years to come.

Another burden was added to Leonard's load in 1928 when it was announced that a Stone & Webster subsidiary holding company, Engineers Public Service Company, was acquiring all the Puget Sound Power & Light Company stock ("Traction" had been eliminated from the name) in exchange for the holding company's shares. Many of the stockholders undoubtedly welcomed this improvement in the diversity of their investment risk. But to some people in Seattle, particularly the adversary press, it was yet another sign of domination by

eastern interests represented by Leonard, the local "villain."

But the overload that finally broke both axles on Leonard's career wagon was the action of Washington

Ole Hanson, Mayor of Seattle at the time of the streetcar system sale.   **Courtesy of the Museum of History & Industry**

A graphic from Puget Power's 1924 annual report shows the company's capacity staying slightly ahead of growing demand.

state voters in passing on November 4, 1930 the District Power Bill, enabling the formation of County Public Utility Districts (with right of condemnation) to enter the electricity distribution business. This came as a major shock to his eastern mentors. Through the well-publicized political build-up to this event, Leonard had no doubt assured them that goodwill toward the company, and the impact of his personal diplomacy, would defuse the issue. Now he argued that these same resources would keep the Act from being implemented. That didn't wash in Boston. Something had gone off the track besides the streetcars! Had Leonard, possibly preoccupied with favorable operating figures, failed to see a change in community sentiment? Had Leonard's style gone out of style? Was public distaste over the eastern control syndrome more than Leonard or anyone else could overcome? Whatever the answers to those questions, the decision of the Board of Directors was that new leadership was called for.

The folklore version of what followed seems right out of a grade-B comedy. Leonard left on his usual vacation, sailing Canadian waters aboard the *Electra*. Upon his return,

Downtown Seattle, in the '20s, looking south on 2nd Avenue: Cars share the road with streetcar tracks.

so the story goes, he found he had no desk, no secretary, no office: He had been replaced by a new president quickly dispatched from Engineers Public Service Company, owners (since 1928) of essentially all the common stock. The documented records of key dates and events cast doubt on the accuracy of that colorful picture, but the fact of Leonard's replacement is certain. The Board of Directors, attempting to save Leonard embarrassment, elected him ceremonial Chairman of the Board; nonetheless, he was understandably crushed. He departed for several months in Europe to get a change of scene and pace. When he returned, rested and renewed, he demonstrated that sense of loyalty exhibited by many long-term employees of Puget Power, by offering his assistance in whatever ways might help the new administration—a pledge he faithfully carried out. He also resigned his recently-acquired but patently token title of Chairman.

Another application of farm electrification: Contented cows, soothed by music from the radio, give better milk, according to a 1930 Puget Sound Electric Journal. [The Journal *was a monthly published by Puget Power and subsidiary companies for their employees.]*

Photo by Asahel Curtis
Courtesy of the Washington State Historical Society

63

Frank McLaughlin

A Word of Appreciation

THE acceptance by the majority of those who voted upon Initiative to the Legislature No. 1, the so-called District Power Bill, was naturally disappointing to all of the employes of our company. We sincerely believed that the passage of this bill was not for the best interest of the people of the State of Washington. If we continue to gain the confidence of the public the effect on the company will be unimportant.

Some of the proponents of this measure stated that in voting for it one was "merely creating a club with which to hold the power company in check." We hope this company has never needed, and does not now need, to be clubbed into doing everything within its power for its customers.

It always has been the policy of the company to sell electric energy to its customers at the lowest possible rates, and to render the best service we know how to render, and we will continue this policy. Important reductions in rates already have been announced to take place in 1931 and 1932, and these reductions will become effective as scheduled.

A proposition has just been made to the stockholders of the company which will, with its acceptance, result in the investment by Engineers Service Company of $5,000,000 in the common stock of Puget ... This amount will partly finance the ... and will improve

64

CHAPTER 7

The gathering storm

I am the Boss!
That was the clear message delivered to employees and stockholders alike when James Francis McLaughlin took over the company presidency on May 1, 1931. He was extending a strong hand, and there can be no doubt that was needed at this critical point in the history of the company. The president's immediate problems included:

- The national business depression, which was causing falling revenues and increased collection problems.

- The low employee morale — in large part due to passage of the District Power Bill, an issue against which the entire company "family" had battled hard.

- The prospect that the Public Utility Districts (PUDs), portended by the District Power Bill, might impede the ability of the company to finance new construction.

- The declared intention of the Bremerton City Council to take over the company's distribution system at the expiration of the current franchise in 1931.

- The default by the City of Seattle on payments on the streetcar revenue bonds it had issued to Puget Power to purchase the system.

- The public image of the company promulgated by the press, as a firm controlled by absentee profiteers in far-off Boston.

Frank McLaughlin, as he preferred to be known, was, like his predecessor Leonard, a veteran of the Stone & Webster "farm team" system of management training. He had started as an office boy, an opportunity created out of the favorable impression he had made as a golf caddy to a Stone & Webster executive. His rapid progress had included tours of duty at Beaumont (Texas) Electric Co.; El Paso Electric Co.; Baton Rouge Electric Co.; Vice President Operations, Virginia Electric Power Co., and later president of the same company; and, in 1930, operating executive of Stone & Webster Service Corporation. McLaughlin had

neither formal training nor experience in the professions of accounting, finance or engineering, then the classical prerequisites for utility company executive postions. But, he had acquired superior communication skills both as a speaker and a writer, and it was these strengths that he used in establishing a new management style at Puget Power. These were also the tools he used to overcome the frequent first impression that he was very young (36) for such high office.

With his opening message McLaughlin meant to strike a blow at the "absentee control" image. "The management contract with Stone &

Webster had been cancelled," he said; "henceforth all management decisions would be made locally," by him. That was technically correct; the management contract had been terminated. It was also true that nearly all the common stock of the company was owned by Engineer's Public Service Company, a Stone & Webster subsidiary holding company where McLaughlin's principal mentor, William Wood, was executive vice president. These two individuals maintained for several years a weekly personal correspondence, on which McLaughlin relied heavily for counsel and home-base support. Wood endorsed McLaughlin's insistance

Rallies of the out-of-work masses were symptomatic of the Great Depression. This gathering occurred Feb. 10, 1931 in front of Seattle's County-City Building, just a few blocks from Puget Power headquarters.

that several western Washington business leaders be elected to the Board of Directors, and this important step was accomplished.

McLaughlin's strategy was to reduce dependency on close liaison with political leaders and legislative bodies. He substituted a greatly expanded program of communication within the company and to the public. Employees were dramatically reminded of the great importance of each individual's job and performance in delivering improved customer service. His favorite speech to employees contained the parable of the bricklayer who, unlike fellow employees, saw his job as not just laying bricks but as building a great cathedral. Customers and the general public were frequently reminded, through McLaughlin's public speeches and published articles, of the company's determination to serve customers on the basis of fair rates. In the fashion of an early day Lee Iacocca, he appealed to the public's sense of fair play in appraising this free-enterprise company's uphill, struggle against the rising clamor for public takeover.

Valiant as McLaughlin's efforts to raise employee morale were, they were repeatedly offset by a series of necessary salary cuts and layoffs. With the Depression-ravaged operation producing no return to shareholders, he had no choice in those bleak mid-1930s.

As for the public power takeover struggle, though its origins dated

"WHAT ARE YOU DOING?" was asked of some workers.

"Laying brick," one replied.

"Making twelve dollars a day," answered the second.

But the third, gazing upward at the rising majesty of the mighty pile, replied:

ROCK ISLAND PLANT

"Building a Great Cathedral!"

THE HUMBLE WORKMAN VISIONED THE GLORIOUS WHOLE; SUCH IS OUR IDEAL IN BUILDING OUR ORGANIZATION FOR BROADER AND MORE CONSTRUCTIVE PUBLIC SERVICE

By FRANK McLAUGHLIN, President
PUGET SOUND POWER & LIGHT CO.

WE, TOO, are carrying bricks; we, too, are engaged in the business of earning a living, and like the third workman, we feel that we are also "building a great cathedral." Ours is an ever rising structure of public service that brightens lives, increases happiness, multiplies man-power and motivates industry throughout the rich and rapidly developing territory which it is the privilege of the Puget Sound Power & Light Company to serve.

Not alone for today, not alone for next year must our plans be laid to meet the electrical needs of our domestic, commercial, industrial and agricultural customers. Far into future years must this program be charted to care adequately and efficiently for an increasing population, growing industries and a greater public service.

We in this organization fully recognize this responsibility, which is placed squarely upon our shoulders. Our management must be the active, vital force which takes men, money and material and puts them to work to render a useful service for the benefit of the public who buys, of the in-

vestor who advances the money, and the employee who labors for the success of the enterprise. Successfully fulfilling our obligation means that:

The people we serve should obtain courteous, prompt, reliable and efficient service at the lowest possible cost;

Those who put their money in the enterprise should receive a fair return on their investment;

Our employees should have a high degree of technical skill; they should be in complete harmony with our ideals of public service; they should be good citizens whom you are delighted to have as neighbors and friends; and they should be fairly compensated for the work they do.

This is the cathedral we are building. And as we build we join with the people of the entire state in constructing another cathedral—a greater state of Washington—a mighty edifice of rich resources, of great industries and of useful institutions—the home, workshop, and playground of a happy people.

PUGET SOUND POWER & LIGHT COMPANY

66

from early company history, its size and pace now grew with a series of federal, state and local events. Nearly 40 years of history had led up to the situation McLaughlin faced.

The Public Power Movement

As early as 1893 Tacoma citizens had expressed dissatisfaction with their water system, operated by Tacoma Light and Power Company. They voted to buy it and immediately began to expand its electric system in competition with Seattle-Tacoma Power Company, a company that later became part of Puget Power. Tacoma City Light built a number of hydroelectric and steam generating plants. Using extremely low residential rates and punitive taxes, they forced Puget Power out of all but a few of its Tacoma commercial and industrial customers. In 1930 the city refused to renew the franchise of Puget Power, and the company had to sell out.

When Seattle Electric Company had been organized in 1900 and its president, Jacob Furth, applied for a 50-year franchise in 1902, he encountered opposition. A Seattle Committee of One Hundred formed, opposing the franchise and proposing that Seattle assume municipal ownership of the electric utility system. Their efforts were not successful, but opposition continued. In 1905 Seattle built a generator at Cedar Falls Dam, the city's principal water supply. Seattle immediately took over the street lighting system and began to build distribution lines parallel to and competing with those of the private power company. In 1912 the city built four miles of track and went into the streetcar business.

In 1911 J.D. Ross had been named Superintendent of Seattle City Light. He came from Ontario, and, as a disciple of public power, approached his work with the zeal of a missionary, determined to build one of the

dominant public power systems in the United States. Throughout his 27-year career with Seattle City Light, J.D. Ross waged a relentless campaign against private power. He was a clever politician who developed the support of the people as well as that of City Council. From the state legislature he secured the right to extend

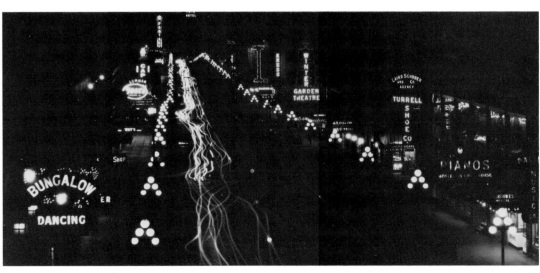

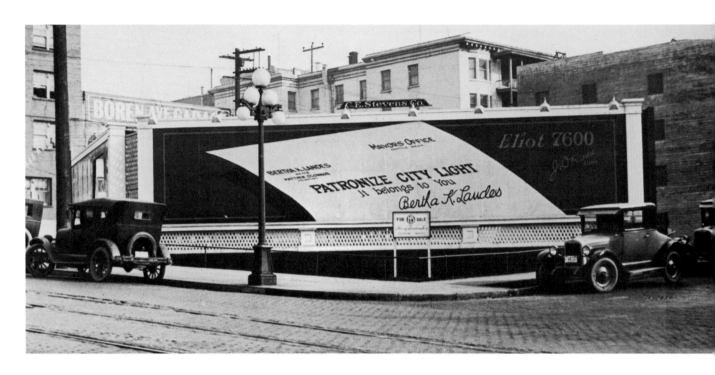

power lines outside city limits, using this to conduct an aggressive campaign to take over Puget Power customers. He campaigned through speeches, news conferences and editorials in local newspapers, never coming directly to Puget Power with any proposal. At various times he recommended that the City Council authorize Seattle City Light to buy out Puget Power, and that it condemn and buy major generating plants such as Snoqualmie Falls, Electron and White River.

The most determined antagonist of Puget Power in Tacoma was Homer T. Bone, who arrived from Indiana in 1899. While employed as a postal clerk he read law at night, passing the Washington State Bar Examination as a self-taught attorney. Bone was an eloquent orator and

courtroom lawyer. A politician with a photographic memory for names and faces, he was ambitious for leadership and power. Bone was first elected to the Washington State Legislature in 1922, serving until 1932.

In 1922 Bone promoted Initiative No. 44, which would have permitted cities to engage in all kinds of business. The voters turned it down. In 1924 he co-sponsored the Reed Bill, which would have permitted cities to extend their electric service beyond city limits, but this failed in the legislature. In 1926 Bone's reintroduction of the Reed Bill as Initiative No. 52 became known as the "Bone Free Power Bill." It provided that municipal power systems could not be taxed and that they could extend their lines beyond city limits and take customers away

from private power companies. State voters turned it down.

Bone changed his tactics. He teamed up with the Washington State Grange and stumped the state, cultivating the farm vote. He rewrote his bill to provide for public utility districts along county lines. It was submitted in 1929 to the state legislature, which failed to act, automatically referring it to the voters at the next general election. The stock market crash intervened on October 29, 1929; and the following year, on November 4, 1930, the Bone District Power Bill was approved by Washington voters—152,000 for and 131,000 against. It is now identified as Chapter 1, Laws of 1931, and is the basis for establishing Public Utility Districts and giving them authority to take over private power company facilities.

Now came dramatic change at the federal level, ushered in by the sweeping victory of Franklin D. Roosevelt, who was elected President in 1932. The same election tide carried Homer T. Bone into office as junior U.S. Senator from the State of Washington. One of the fundamental changes on the agenda of the new administration was to advocate public power as an instrument of social change.

Federal actions began with authorizing the Army Corps of Engineers and the Bureau of Reclamation to build large dams on major rivers. These dams had several purposes: navigation, flood control, recreation, wildlife refuge and "other purposes," which was a euphemism for power generation. Only a portion of the cost of these dams was allocated to power generation, and the amount to be repaid to the United States Treasury was set up on a 50-year amortization at two percent interest. This provided extremely low cost power, and Congress promptly enacted a public preference clause giving all public power agencies first call on this power.

Construction of Muscle Shoals Dam on the Tennessee River at Florence, Alabama, occasioned the creation of the Tennessee Valley Authority, an agency that covered about 41,000 square miles in parts of seven states. Established in 1933, TVA eventually took over all of the private power companies in its defined territory. With apparently similar goals Bone introduced a bill in Congress to authorize a Columbia River Authority, but it did not pass. He then introduced legislation to form the Bonneville Power Administration, which would market the power from a number of federal dams along the Columbia River. This was approved in 1938. Bonneville Dam on the Columbia River was authorized, and construction began

69

in 1933, with completion in 1937. Grand Coulee Dam was authorized, and construction began in 1935, with completion in 1942.

The Rural Electrification Act was established by Presidential Order in 1935 and approved by Congress in 1936, becoming part of the responsibilities of the Department of Agriculture. REA provided for loans up to 35 years and at two percent interest, to extend electric power to farms. This money was not available to established investor-owned utilities, only to public (cooperative owned) power groups formed for the purpose. These became known as REA Cooperatives.

Each of these extensions of federal authority further fueled the activities of PUD and municipal power advocates in Washington state, but not in a unifying way. The PUD proponents saw the advent of federally subsidized dams, coupled with legislation giving preference to public power distributors, as the means to take over the service territories of investor-owned utilities. Municipal utility advocates were torn between their interest in subsidized power and their concerns that a combination of federal and county PUD forces might dominate their independent plans. The one common ground of these two groups was the goal of dismembering Puget Power. The rallying cry was usually that "this God-given water power resource belonged to all the people — not the utility barons." But those who said this didn't note that you couldn't drop the cords on your toaster and coffee pot into the nearest stream and get a free breakfast.

McLaughlin took his appeal for recognition of the unfairness of tax-subsidized government competition in business to every audience he could find or create. His theme was the inequity of government, at any level, launching a utility business operation permitted to use tax-exempt financing and exempt from paying the usual property taxes and vehicle license fees. His articles on this subject pointing up the latent threat to all free enterprise attracted national attention and favorable comment from Merryl S. Rukeyser, B.C. Forbes, and William Hard of the Reader's Digest.

Initially, McLaughlin had some successes. Bremerton reversed its takeover stance and renewed the Puget Power franchise in 1931. Puyallup dropped its first condemnation suit in 1931. PUD elections in Snohomish, Skagit, Whatcom and Island Counties were defeated in 1932. McLaughlin was applauded at Stone & Webster for this indication of his persuasiveness; but soon was again hammered over the company's dismal financial results. First common

Bonneville Dam

Courtesy of the
Washington State
Historical Society

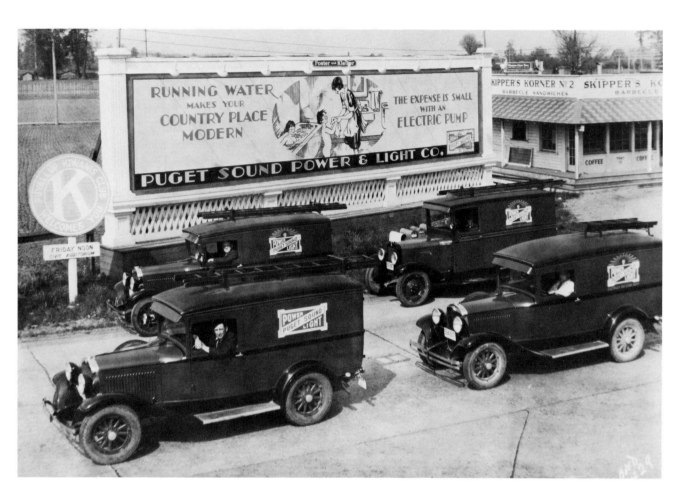

Above: Service fleet and billboard, Puyallup, in the early '30s.

Left: The Puyallup local office of Puget Power, a classic of the art deco style, was built in 1929.

stock and then even preferred stock dividends had to be suspended.

In spite of everything McLaughlin could do, the clouds shadowing Puget Power's future became ever thicker and darker:

- In 1933 the state legislature authorized municipal systems to extend their lines beyond city limits without regulation or the payment of offsetting taxes.

- In 1934 the City of Seattle began to enlist the aid of investment bankers to press its Puget Power takeover effort.

- In November 1936 nine of the nineteen counties served by Puget Power voted to form PUDs.

- In 1938 four more of the counties served by Puget Power voted formation of PUDs, for a total of thirteen. King and Pierce Counties were notable exceptions, largely because Seattle and Tacoma municipal utilities vigorously opposed the formation of countywide PUDs.

- In the late 1930s the ever-deepening threat to the service area and revenue base of the company had made the financing of new construction nearly impossible.

Second floor lobby of the Puget Power Building, Seattle, March, 1930.

Through this darkening picture McLaughlin maintained his posture of courage and confidence. The battle was being fought in terms of political philosophy and ownership interest. It is particularly noteworthy that at no time did the company's adversaries attempt to make a case based on deficiency of Puget Power's power supply or a lack of reliability or quality of the company's service. Clearly the rank-and-file employees were doing their jobs. True, in 1934, as authorized by the federal National Recovery Administration Act, Puget Power employees voted to organize as a bargaining unit of the International Brotherhood of Electrical Workers union. This replacement of the employees' Mutual Benefit Association caused no interruption

in customer service.

The onset of World War II brought a temporary truce in the public power takeover war. The federal government mandated power pooling to best serve the huge increases in war industry demand. This forced an unaccustomed degree of cooperative

Puget Power linemen in front of Seattle line-room (now the site of the Medical-Dental Building in downtown Seattle). Some of the men in this 1910 photo were involved in the earliest efforts toward formal representation of electrical workers. **Top row, from left:** William Dick, E.M. Bird, (?) Snow, Roy Heckathorn, John Ridley, George Stocks, (?) Jones, Carl Duley, (?) McClaffety. **Bottom row:** Fred DeSylvia, George Jackman, C.E. Bird holding Rags the Dog, Dan Trink, Jim Perry, (?) Hamm.

effort among the publicly-owned and investor-owned utilities. Also the availability of capital to finance takeover efforts evaporated. As the "power war" underwent an armistice, the burdens of the real war began to be felt in very human terms. The call to military service was answered by 577 Puget Power employees, of whom over 50 were wounded and 13 killed. Those remaining on the job found countless ways to do double duty.

Midway through the World War II years, a long-smoldering utility industry fire was extinguished, with important consequences to the future of Puget Power.

Puget Power employees were justly proud of their support of the King County Defense Chest in 1941.
On the stage, from left: *Anne Nievinski, Tom Sawyer, Bob Tucker, Guy Kienholz, Fritz Fall, Bill Biggs, Jim Spellar, Doug Boone, Tex Lewis, Rog Walker, Tom Arnold, Fred Maydole, John Wallin, Margaret McGill, Elaine Albin, Harry Martin, Leonard Schneider, Clyde Millar, Bob Carlson, Harold Abramson, Al Stewart, Bill Stanaway.*
Back row: *Grace Weckwerth, Dorothy McClellan, Henry Hardin, Louis Krull, Manley Brown, Henry Kruse, W.L. Robbins. (Foreground figures unidentified)*

Behold *THE POWER TRUST*

YOU have heard tales about a so-called "Power Trust" —of its devilment, its racketeering, its greedy exploitation of the users of electric service. You have been told that this awful menace to public welfare should be stamped out—absolutely crushed. Naturally your curiosity has been aroused and no doubt you have wanted to see a picture of the terrible octopus. Well, here it is. Not what you expected at all, is it? You have been mystified before, maybe you are now surprised to see this picture of the "Power Trust"; revealing who the owners of the company really are—among them your friends and neighbors. These are the folks who invested in power facilities because they had faith in and trusted the public to give them a square deal. Over 40,000 institutions and individuals have put their money in this property. Many additional thousands are indirectly affected through holdings of bonds and stocks by commercial and savings banks, insurance companies, churches, schools, colleges, religious societies, charitable associations, hospitals, children's and old folk's homes and the like.

Frank M Laughlin
PRESIDENT

PUGET SOUND POWER & LIGHT COMPANY

One of a series of ads run by Puget Power in 1935 to counteract public power advocates' effort to paint investor-owned power companies as greedy and oppressive.

The old State Capitol building in Olympia, pictured here in 1912, was the scene of much heated debate as anti-private power sentiments grew during the '20s. (A new capitol was opened in 1928.)

Courtesy of the Museum of History & Industry

Penalized for holding: the feds blow the whistle

The last thing McLaughlin needed was another major problem—but there it was! At least that's the way he remembered that day, August 26, 1935, when Congress had passed the Utility Holding Company Act. The thrust of that Act was to require companies that owned controlling stock in several geographically unrelated utilities to dispose of those interests, returning each utility to the status of an independent firm. Engineers Public Service Company qualified as a holding company, and that meant its Puget Power common stock would have to be sold. Under the rising threat of public power takeover, Puget Power common stock had already become a less than attractive investment. Now, just as McLaughlin was struggling to hold the company together, this legislation dictated a forced sale. Would this require a sudden change in strategy? What had he done to deserve this?

Of course, neither he nor Puget Power had done anything to precipitate this event. However, a chain of events that began with the formation of the Seattle Electric Light Co. and similar infant utilities around the country had finally spawned what Congress now viewed as monsters for the slaying.

When Sidney Mitchell had launched Seattle Electric Light Co. in 1886, and similar companies in the region shortly thereafter, he soon encountered a fundamental problem that plagues the industry to this very day: How to raise the capital to finance new plants needed to meet the ever-growing demand for more electric service? Thomas Edison had not made matters any easier by his insistence from the start that all equipment must be paid for with cash on delivery! The capital requirements were substantially greater than for most other industries — approximately $5 of new investment for each additional $1 of annual revenue from service. Such amounts could not be raised out of current competitive rates on a pay-as-you-go basis. This limitation was sharply defined when the Washington Public Service Commission was formed in 1911, and adopted the principle that electric rates could not exceed sums necessary to recover legitimate operating costs (at cost) plus a reasonable return on the existing required investment.

Frenetic trading on the New York Stock Exchange, whose crash on October 29, 1929 precipitated the Great Depression.

Courtesy of the Bettmann Archive

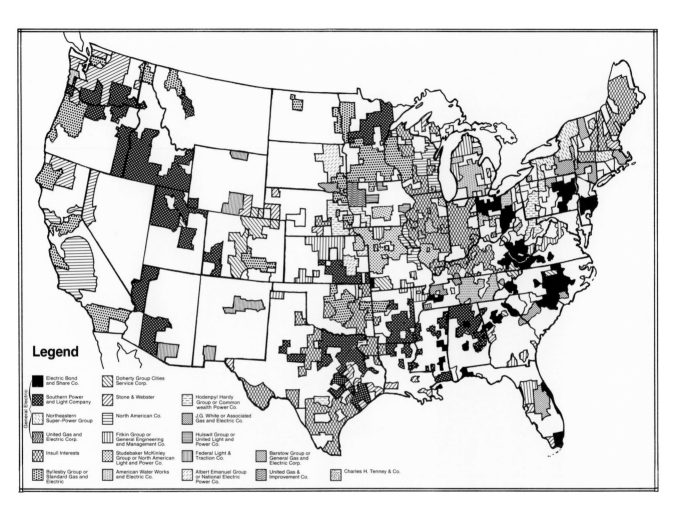

Legend

General Electric

- Electric Bond and Share Co.
- Southern Power and Light Company
- Northeastern Super-Power Group
- United Gas and Electric Corp.
- Insull Interests
- Byllesby Group or Standard Gas and Electric

- Doherty Group Cities Service Corp.
- Stone & Webster
- North American Co.
- Fitkin Group or General Engineering and Management Co.
- Studebaker McKinley Group or North American Light and Power Co.
- American Water Works and Electric Co.

- Hodenpyl Hardy Group or Commonwealth Power Co.
- J.G. White or Associated Gas and Electric Co.
- Hulswit Group or United Light and Power Co.
- Federal Light & Traction Co.
- Albert Emanuel Group or National Electric Power Co.

- Barstow Group or General Gas and Electric Corp.
- United Gas & Improvement Co.
- Charles H. Tenney & Co.

Fields of operation of major electric utility holding companies, in 1925. Note the Stone & Webster holdings dominating the Northwest region. The Utility Holding Company Act of 1935 led to the companies' divestiture of individual utilities, including Puget Power.

The electric utility industry at first followed the general pattern of capital structure developed earlier in the railroad industry:

Common Stock	20%
Preferred Stock	20%
Debt	60%
TOTAL	100%

However, this pattern alone did not solve two problems unique to the electric utility industry: First, because of the basic interdependency of all parts of an electric network, it was not acceptable to place mortgages securing different debt borrowings on separate parts of the system. His experience with the predecessor units of Puget Power showed Sidney Mitchell that a new financing tool was needed: the open-end mortgage. With the help of New England financing institutions, he was able to adapt earlier railroad industry practices to provide such a tool. Under this scheme each unit of new construction (lines, buildings, generating plants) is automatically added to the assets covered by a "master mortgage" securing all of the company's bonded indebtedness.

The second problem was how to attract the required common stock investment. Around the turn of the century, the electric utility industry in general — and the budding little electric companies in particular — were regarded as high-risk investments, surprising as that may seem for a growth industry. Even as dedicated a venture capitalist as J.P. Morgan at first refused to provide Thomas Edison the capital to build a plant to mass-produce incandescent bulbs. The prevailing feeling at the time was that the somewhat more secure preferred stock in the local utility company could probably be sold to local investors (this proved to be the case); but the common stock could be marketed only to wealthy speculators seeking high-risk returns. How was that sort of investor, then found chiefly in the northeastern part of the country, to be attracted to invest in such faroff frontiers as western Washington?

The Holding Company

By the late 1890s Sidney Mitchell, Stone & Webster and others were developing an answer: the electric utility syndications that later took the form of the holding company. Here is a very simplified model:

ELECTRIC HOLDING CO.

$1 . . . . Common Stock
$1 . . . . Preferred Stock
$3 . . . . Debt
_____
$5 . . . . CAPITAL

USED TO ACQUIRE

	Utility A	Utility B	Utility C	Utility D	Utility E
Common Stock	$1	$1	$1	$1	$1
Preferred Stock	$1	$1	$1	$1	$1
Debt	$3	$3	$3	$3	$3
TOTAL CAPITAL	$5	$5	$5	$5	$5

"Electric Holding Co." was formed to own all of the common (voting)

Businessman John Pierpont Morgan's name came to symbolize capitalism.

Courtesy of the
Bettmann Archive

stock of, say, five electric utilities. The investment of the $1 in common stock of the holding company carried considerably less risk than the investment of the same $1 in the common stock of any one of the electric utilities. This was particularly so if the electric utilities were located in widely separated regions with differing economies and climates.

This financing tool was an instant success in facilitating the formation of the large amounts of capital needed to finance the rapidly growing electric utility industry. With that growth came prosperity to many companies and individuals. As one example, Sidney Mitchell became president of EBASCO, initially a subsidiary of

General Electric Co., but later the independent center of a worldwide network of engineering service and utility holding companies. Nearly all of the electric utilities in the Pacific Northwest except Puget Power became affiliated with EBASCO. Puget Power, in company with Virginia Electric Power Co. and numerous other utilities, became part of the Stone & Webster network. Eight or more other holding company networks were similarly formed.

In its most innocent form, the holding company provided the legitimate functions of a modern-day electric utility mutual fund. Necessary equity capital was raised at risk levels more attractive to many

investors than otherwise possible. That sort of innocence was short-lived however: Capitalists motivated less by concern for reliable electric service than by old-fashioned greed were attracted by other features of the holding company model. Through its voting power, $1 of holding company stock (in our example) provided control over all $25 of utility assets.

A meeting of Stone & Webster officials, Baker River, May, 1925. **From left:** *George P. Jessup, H.B. Sewall, E.W. Purdy, Edwin S. Webster,* *W.D. Shannon, C.W. Howard, A.W. Leonard, D.C. Barnes, F.S. Pratt, Charles A. Stone, Sam Shuffleton.*

If that was not enough leverage, think what fun one could have with a super holding company owning, say, five holding companies! That's exactly the sort of thing that happened. And with that kind of power the possibilities for mischief were almost limitless. For instance, the services of holding company affiliates in the engineering, construction, accounting, and insurance fields could be forced on utility subsidiaries at whatever fees the traffic would bear. The utility operating costs could be artifically increased by all sorts of charges for financing, consulting and other services. Utility commission attempts to control some of these practices were at first frustrated when courts ruled that their authority did not extend to control of the holding companies.

The Utility Holding Company Act

Finally in 1928, public outcry over the abuses of the holding company structure attracted federal attention in the form of a Federal Trade Commission investigation. The result, seven years later (and after the spectacular failure of Samuel Insull's holding company empire, Insull Utility Investments, Inc.), was the Utility Holding Company Act of 1935. Though as president of Puget Power he was the "nominee" of a holding company — Engineers Public Service Company — McLaughlin adopted the positive

stance that implementation of the act with the sale of Puget Power stock would be a favorable step toward local ownership and stronger state regulation, which he approved.

Implementation did not come quickly. Only in 1941, after six years of litigation, did the Supreme Court affirm the constitutionality of the Utility Holding Company Act and confirm the validity of divestiture orders. Even then, what with widespread preoccupation with the problems of World War II, two more years were required for Engineers Public Service Company to complete and obtain appropriate approvals for the specific Puget Power divestiture plan.

Finally on March 16, 1943, the Securities & Exchange Commission approved the plan. Approval of the Department of Public Service of Washington followed directly. The plan covered restructuring Puget Power debt and the resolution of arrearages of dividends due preferred stockholders. But the most important feature was the distribution of the Engineers Public Service Co. interest to holders of Puget Power preferred stock. Controlling ownership of Puget Power thus passed to some 15,000 individual stockholders, approximately 9,400 of whom were Washington state residents.

On December 17, 1943 at a special

Samuel Insull, a leading developer (and later an abuser) of the utility holding company structure; brought down in 1932 when the financial collapse of his overinflated empire brought disaster to millions of investors.

Courtesy of the Bettmann Archive

meeting of stockholders, a new Board of Directors was elected; all eight were residents of western Washington. For the first time in its history, control of Puget Power was in the hands of "home rule." McLaughlin was jubilant!

Above: *Joshua Green, Peoples National Bank of Washington, served on the reorganized Puget Power's Board of Directors from 1943 to 1965. Other members of the company's first "home rule" board: Roy E. Campbell, Arden Farms; Darrah Corbet, Smith Cannery Machines; Uberto Dickey, Soundview Pulp; Philip G. Johnson, Boeing Company; D.K. MacDonald, D.K. MacDonald Co.; Russell* *Miller, Pacific, Gamble, Robinson Co.; and Puget Power executives Frank McLaughlin and William H. McGrath.*

Right: *World War II brought important changes to the work force. Puget Power and many of its major commercial and industrial customers employed an increasing number of women. Here, a team of "Rosie Riveters" are trained for industrial jobs with the Boeing Co.*

CHAPTER 9

A city of two tales

With the World War II victory in 1945 came the opportunity for a new start — for individuals, institutions and businesses. To Puget Power it meant a return to that other war, the public power takeover struggle. The temporary armistice of the past four years had been like the uneasy peace in the eye of a hurricane. Everyone now anxiously awaited the second half of the storm!

Public power vs. private power. Progressives vs. conservatives. Advocates of social reform and government control vs. advocates of "laissez-faire" (hands-off) by government. The local scene had been swept into the national struggle that began in the 1890s and continued into the twentieth century. The battle was fought on two major fronts, one in the city of Seattle, the other in nineteen county service areas.

The Battle for Seattle

Seattle's story is unique. The city's first moves toward public power (already noted in earlier chapters) made it the only major city in the United States that had both its own municipal power system and competing service from a private power company. It seemed an affront to liberals everywhere. The public vs. private power fight in Seattle made the national press. Public power advocates were outraged that the situation was not immediately resolved in favor of the municipal utility.

Above: In 1945, crowds filled Seattle streets to celebrate the end of the war, while (right:) the old war over Seattle electrical service was rekindled.

Courtesy of the Museum of History & Industry

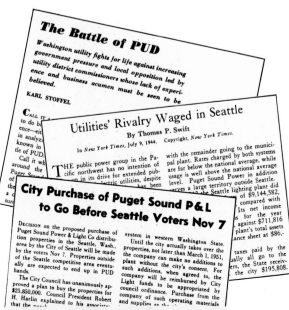

The Battle of PUD

Washington utility fights for life against increasing government pressure and local opposition led by utility district commissioners whose lack of experience and business acumen must be seen to be believed.

KARL STOFFEL

CALL IT A...
to do b...
ence—cit...
in analyz...
known in...
tle of PUD...

Call it wh...
around the...
Puget Sou...
of ... ...ectric utilities, despite
... ...has been

Utilities' Rivalry Waged in Seattle

By Thomas P. Swift

In *New York Times*, July 9, 1944. Copyright, *New York Times*.

THE public power group in the Pacific northwest has no intention of ... up in its drive for extended pub... with the remainder going to the municipal plant. Rates charged by both systems are far below the national average, while usage is well above the national average level. Puget Sound Power in addition serves a large territory outside Seattle.

... ...e Seattle lighting plant did
... ...of $9,144,582,
... ...compared with
... ...Its net income
... ...s for the year
... ...against $711,816
... ...plant's total assets
... ...ance sheet at $86,-

... taxes paid by the
... ...ally all go to the
...rs, the State receiv-
... ...e city $195,808.

City Purchase of Puget Sound P&L to Go Before Seattle Voters Nov 7

DECISION on the proposed purchase of Puget Sound Power & Light Co distribution properties in the Seattle, Wash., area by the City of Seattle will be made by the voters Nov 7. Properties outside of the Seattle competitive area eventually are expected to end up in PUD hands.

The City Council has unanimously approved a plan to buy the properties for $25,850,000. Council President Robert H. Harlin explained to his associates that the pur...

system in western Washington State.
Until the city actually takes over the properties, not later than March 1, 1951, the company can make no additions to plant without the city's consent. For such additions, when agreed to, the company will be reimbursed by City Light funds to be appropriated by council ordinance. Purchase from the company of such operating materials and supplies as th...

84

When Seattle entered the electricity distribution business in 1905, and began to build competitive streetcar lines in 1912, the fight was on. It was waged street by street, alley by alley, house by house and customer by customer. Employees of the private company regularly checked city hall for new building permits, so they could call to offer electric service before ground was broken. They kept a close check on their own neighborhoods and reported when a family moved out or in. Transfer and storage companies were solicited for information on moves.

The municipal system used the same tactics and added a few more. Applicants for city business licenses and developers starting new subdivisions were "energetically encouraged" to choose City Light electric service.

In 1916 City Engineer R. H. Thompson made the first serious suggestion that the city acquire Puget Power. He proposed a $10 million bond issue to purchase the company's city properties and its Snoqualmie Falls power plant. The plan never came to a vote of the city council.

Much of the public vs. private power battle was a propaganda war fought on the front pages of Seattle's

Annual Report for 1949

PUGET SOUND POWER & LIGHT COMPANY

Left: Duplication of distribution facilities was an often-cited argument for Seattle City Light's proposed takeover of Puget Power's Seattle holdings.

Courtesy of Seattle City Light

Above: The cover of Puget Power's 1949 annual report reflected the company's frustration and anxiety over the public power onslaught.

and the nation's newspapers. The Seattle Star sided with Seattle City Light and almost always favored anything suggested by that utility. J.D. Ross was a frequent contributor, through interviews, editorials and feature articles under his own by-line. The Seattle Times supported Puget Power. The Times carried articles favorable to the company and ran an occasional letter-to-the-editor from Frank McLaughlin. The Seattle Post-Intelligencer was inclined toward neutrality, was relatively objective, and found something good to say about both City Light and Puget Power.

The Years with Ross

William O'Dell Sparks, in an unpublished master's thesis dated 1964 (University of Washington), emphasizes the importance of the struggle in Seattle saying:

The genius of public ownership in the State of Washington has occurred in Seattle. The ideas had been carefully nurtured and defended by the Superintendent of the Seattle plant, J.D. Ross. And the public power movement owed a great deal to Ross for its eventual success. For it was Ross who supplied the movement with a goodly number of its basic ideas and techniques. Seattle is one of the most crucial battlegrounds in the nationwide fight between the advocates of public ownership and the entrenched interests of private industry.

Seattle's daily newspapers, the Times, the Post-Intelligencer and the Star, played distinct and critical roles in the struggle between Puget Power and Seattle City Light.

Photos courtesy of the Museum of History & Industry

86

The National Electric Light Association shared this sense of importance, and is reported by Sparks to have written:

The Seattle situation is of national importance. At a time when activities are being made to extend the business of Government into other localities, the claim of successful results of such a policy in Seattle is dangerous and requires refutation.

The struggle continued through the 1920s. Now and again, usually at the time of his annual report to the City Council, Superintendent J.D. Ross would suggest that the city acquire the Seattle properties of Puget Power, together with its generating facilities at Georgetown, Snoqualmie Falls, White River and Electron. Ross publicized these offers through the Seattle Star but never directly approached the company.

In January, 1930 the Post-Intelligencer predicted that Seattle would probably attempt to condemn the Seattle distribution system of Puget Power and its White River generating plant, quoting a member of the Seattle City Council as saying that two ordinances had been drafted for this purpose. The Star was in complete agreement with the proposal. The Times did not comment.

On October 3, 1934, Ross announced his plan for the City of Seattle to acquire all of Puget Power. Until now he had proposed to acquire only the company's

Seattle City Light Superintendent J.D. Ross in 1931, three years before announcing his ill-fated plan to take over the entire Puget Power system.

Courtesy of the Museum of History & Industry

Seattle system. Now his stated plan was to put Puget Power out of business forever.

Seattle would acquire the entire Puget Power system, from the Canadian border to the Columbia River, including all of the counties on Puget Sound and many of those in central Washington. The price was set at $95 million, to be financed by a 30-year bond issue at five percent interest. Seattle would then sell to other municipals and public utility

districts that wanted their own share of the system.

Ross enlisted the aid of Guy Myers, a former employee of Montana Power Company and a well-known go-between with eastern investment bankers, to form a financing scheme for his plan. When Myers' negotiating offer was "waved off" by McLaughlin, he tried to go directly to Stone & Webster, but received no encouragement there.

Ross found little support on the

City Council. The Times completely opposed the plan. The Post-Intelligencer reported it in detail, but emphasized the opposition. Even the Star, always a Ross supporter, could not endorse this takeover plan.

More opposition came from the cities of Bremerton, Bellingham, Everett and Yakima, the Association of Washington Cities, and all of the counties in eastern and central Washington affected by his proposal. Many regarded it as an attempt by Ross to get cheap power from Bonneville and Grand Coulee that would be marketed in western Washington. Many more said they didn't want to take over Puget Power and were willing to continue the company's service. Even Homer T. Bone refused to endorse this latest Ross proposal.

Within a few days Ross acknowledged the violent opposition to his plan and said he was willing to confine the takeover to the Puget Power system in Seattle and King County. This did not help much. The opposition continued to blast the original proposal. The issue faded from Seattle newspapers by the end of 1934. There was still talk, but little action. In August, 1935 Franklin D. Roosevelt appointed J.D. Ross to the Federal Securities and Exchange Commission, and Ross departed from the local scene. With his departure, his plan simply faded away.

But that did not end the concept

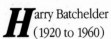

J.D. Ross (right) receives congratulations from Seattle Mayor Charles L. Smith in 1936, after leaving Seattle City Light for federal service.

Courtesy of the Museum of History & Industry

of a City Light takeover of Puget Power within Seattle. Indeed, by November 1943 the Seattle City Council adopted a resolution to expand its power generating capacity with the intention of taking over service to Puget Power's Seattle customers at the expiration of the company's 50-year franchise in 1952.

The Battle is Joined

Now, after the war, as things got back to "normal," the battle tactics got increasingly serious. Customers were "stolen" back and forth, accompanied by midnight and weekend "cutovers." Today's "60 Minutes" TV crews would have had a field day with the story.

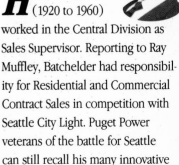

Harry Batchelder

Harry Batchelder (1920 to 1960) worked in the Central Division as Sales Supervisor. Reporting to Ray Muffley, Batchelder had responsibility for Residential and Commercial Contract Sales in competition with Seattle City Light. Puget Power veterans of the battle for Seattle can still recall his many innovative and aggressive ways of securing customer contracts for service.

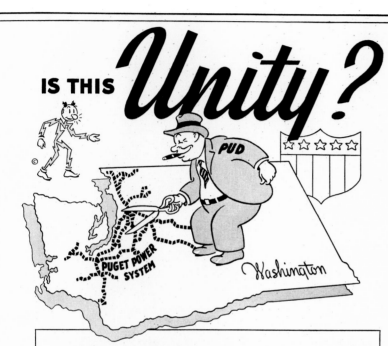

IS THIS *Unity?*

DEDICATED TO NATIONAL DEFENSE **PUGET POWER**

PUGET SOUND POWER & LIGHT COMPANY

MORE than three-quarters of a century ago when this nation faced a serious crisis, America's great leader, Abraham Lincoln came forth with his plea, which was also a warning: "United we stand; divided we fall." Today, when another great emergency faces us, our leaders come forward with this same plea of UNITY—and the hearts and minds of all thinking Americans echo in unison—"They are right!"

We must have UNITY in this Country or the day will come when we have NOTHING. Our number one problem is UNITY for National Defense—let's have it.

And, while on this subject, let me say Puget Power stands prepared and willing to do its share in maintaining and defending the American Way of Life. We have an organization of 2750 men and women who understand the order, "Forward March!" better than any other in the catalogue—and behind them is an array of mechanized equipment second to none. We have a closely knit, well integrated system which pools the energy of fifteen power plants, interconnected by 11,000 miles of service line.

All this in itself is a picture of UNITY—400,000 horse power merged into a single controlled force for the common good, and nearly 5,000 units of human power made up of men and women devoted to the highest ideals of public welfare.

Anyone who would cut up this system is attacking the very principle which is admitted to be the guiding need of these times. We can't get UNITY by destroying UNITY. Those who would apply the wire cutters to Puget Power for the purpose of dividing it into nineteen or any other number of separate parts are serving WEAKNESS to this nation on a platter—and don't forget it.

Puget Power is a product of free American Enterprise dedicated to the Defense of America. As such, it should be preserved!

Frank M. Laughlin
President

The war years provided an opportunity for Puget Power to express the need for unity in opposition to the divisiveness represented by public power takeover efforts.

Reddy Kilowatt

Reddy Kilowatt may have been the electric utility industry's hardest worker. The idea for Reddy came in 1926 in a literal flash of lightning to Ashton B. Collins, Sr., of Alabama Power Company, who had long sought a symbol for the miracle of electricity.

By 1933, Collins had built his own public relations firm around Reddy, and in 1934 Philadelphia Electric became the first company to adopt the little ambassador of electric service.

Puget Power began using Reddy Kilowatt in its marketing programs in 1937, becoming one of hundreds of electric utilities all over the world to do so.

In the 60s, as aggressive marketing gave way to a new emphasis on conservation and energy efficiency, Puget Power turned to different public relations and advertising concepts. But to more than a generation of Puget Power customers, Reddy Kilowatt personified safe, reliable, innovative electric service.

CONDEMNATION AXE

PUGET POWER SERVICE AREA

Annual Report
for 1950
PUGET SOUND POWER
& LIGHT COMPANY

*The impending loss of
the company's Seattle
service territory set the
tone for the 1950
annual report, pub-
lished in March, 1951
— the month the sale
became final.*

By 1947 McLaughlin had reached the point of exasperation. Customers, he said, were entitled to increased service to meet the needs of the rapidly growing city, its ever-increasing industrial and commercial electricity loads. The threat of City Light takeover made it impractical for Puget Power to finance additional distribution system capacity. And for all the talk and the threats and the council resolutions dating back nearly 50 years, Seattle had never approached the company with a bona fide offer to purchase its portion of the city system. If the city meant to drive Puget Power out by a combination of disabling threats, punitive taxes, and system duplications, that was patently unfair! He appealed to the public sense of fair play, stating that, "either the city should forthwith (in 1947) buy Puget Power's Seattle properties, or it should allow Puget Power to buy City Light." No response.

Finally in 1950, as the end of the franchise approached, Seattle made a formal offer to purchase. On June 30 after serious consideration of both customer and stockholder interests, the Puget Power Board of Directors voted approval — all subject to a favorable vote of the people. The proposed deal became Proposition C on the November 7, 1950 ballot.

The issue was hotly debated, with national news coverage. McLaughlin publicly supported Proposition C, convinced that for the company it was the best of a bad lot

Above: Seattle City Light has been head-quartered in this building at Third and Madison since 1935. In 1957, seven stories were added.

Courtesy of Seattle City Light

Below: In the fall of 1950, having decided to accept a Seattle takeover, Puget Power went to print to urge employees and customers to support the sale.

YOU CANNOT GET JOB SECURITY BY SABOTAGE
By FRANK McLAUGHLIN, President

In the almost 20 years that I have been with Puget, the Company has experienced some rude awakenings and rather severe shocks — which for the most part it has been able to shrug off because of the external origin of the "dynamiters". However, the worst "below the belt" blow Puget has to my knowledge received was the disgraceful and despicable action of some of its Seattle employees in their misguided opposition to Proposition "C".

It is awfully hard to realize that the only attempt to "smear and be-smirch" the Company, in reference to Proposition "C", came largely from employees of Puget, who in the long run have everything and noth-ing to gain by such tactics. They are cutting the...

It is a source of deep regret to me to... find that Puget has on its payr... seemingly determined... selves and their... sacrifice the pub... "bite the hand that... would impugn the... pany and blacken its... conceived selfish i... through a malicious a... ganda campaign, dist... ceived the public—app... by having the ghost of... deal" stalk the ballot bo... —aroused suspicion as t... ting value recei... cha...

Puget Power, City Light Join in Election Campaign

Some $35.000 is being spent in news-paper and radio advertising to convince the citizens of Seattle that they should approve the proposed $25.850,000 mu-nicipal purchase of Puget Sound Power & Light Co properties in the general of alternatives. He asked that all employees join in that support, a request that was apparently not uniformly followed.

Only after the absentee ballots were counted could the outcome be determined: Yes — 65,616; No — 64,892; and over 40,000 of those casting ballots did not vote on Proposition C.

On March 5, 1951 McLaughlin signed the papers completing the sale. The price: $26,834,232 — of which $24,859,123 was required to pay off the related amount of mortgage bond indebtedness.

It was a dark day for Puget Power. Forty percent of the company's revenue base had been lost. The eastern financial community had written the company off. But, Frank McLaughlin knew that things could get worse— and sure enough, they did!

Far right: Puget Power directors and other officials map out plans for Seattle's acquisition of the company's holdings at a work session in 1950.

Right: The condemnation axe, by now a familiar theme, again haunted an annual report cover. In 1951's report, McLaughlin called for a sweeping reexamination of federal domination of the Northwest's electric power picture.

Above: Rock Island Dam became one of the instruments in the federal campaign against investor-owned electric power. This photo shows the facility's fish ladder, an early effort at environmental mitigation.

Right: The war effort provided artistic inspiration for Puget Power's marketing program. The momentum continued into the business boom of the late '40s.

CHAPTER 10

The lively corpse

To many of its adversaries, Puget Power now looked like a staggering, wounded warrior. It was time to move in for the kill!

It was not just the outcome of the battle with Seattle City Light that created this impression. A whole series of events dating back to the early 1940s had served to make the company's future look ever more dismal.

- In 1941 the federal government, acting within the terms of the Rock Island Dam permit, asked the company to add eight generating units to the project. Puget Power was obviously in no position to finance such additions, and the consequential threat was loss of this most valuable resource. The advent of World War II put this matter into abeyance.

- By 1941, eleven years after passage of the District Power Bill, condemnation lawsuits had been filed by ten of the nineteen counties served. There had been no court decisions handed down, no firm PUD offers received, just constant threats and the resulting negative impact on the ability to finance new construction.

- On March 19, 1943 a Seattle federal court jury set at $9.5 million the condemnation price for company property Snohomish County PUD sought to acquire — a price two and one-half times the PUDs estimate. Similarly high awards were handed down in cases relating to Whatcom, Thurston, Lewis, Cowlitz, and Clallam counties. These awards, combined with the war economy, discouraged the PUDs temporarily, and made it possible for the company to refinance $52 million in debt until 1949-50.

- On July 15, 1944 Clallam County PUD chose to proceed under its condemnation award, paying Puget Power $600,000 for its property in that county. This first loss of territory carried with it only one percent of the company's revenue base, but even that loss had ominous overtones.

- Late in 1945 a hint of future events came when representatives of a group of PUDs approached Puget Power with the idea of acquiring the entire company by buying its common stock at the (low) market price. The offer was not backed by any demonstrated ability to carry out the idea and came to naught.

The end of World War II brought on a business boom in western Washington that, to most, was the best of news. Contrary to the power supply glut that many had predicted, a shortage loomed. Puget Power was now in desperate straits to finance even modest extensions of its distribution system, let alone any new generating facilities. In fact, reactivation in 1946 of the federal directive to add generators at Rock Island threatened a major cut in the company's power supply.

Cutaway of a Francis model low-head turbine, typical of the type used at Rock Island Dam during the '40s.

This one was designed and manufactured by Allis-Chalmers Manufacturing Company.

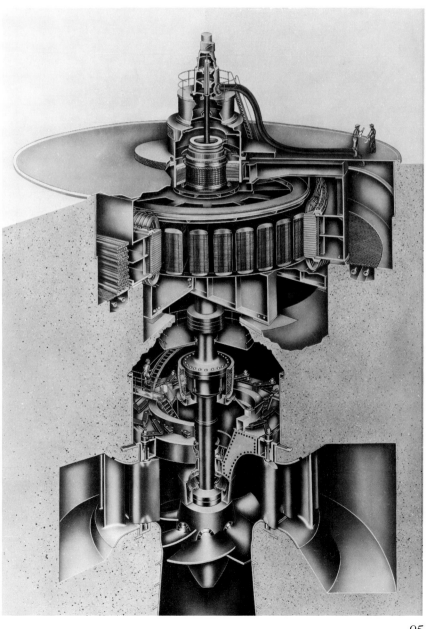

Facing an increasingly desperate situation, McLaughlin resorted to short-term moves that only aggravated outsiders' assessment of the company's future. He began to sell off perimeter territories and non-electric subsidiary operations. The gas systems in Bellingham and Wenatchee and the Vashon Island telephone systems were among the first to go. Even the North Coast Transportation Company, which had contributed important profits toward the meager utility earnings, was sold to Greyhound. In 1948 perimeter electric utility properties (excluding power plants), constituting about 10 percent of the company's customer and revenue base, were sold to eight county PUDs: Chelan, Douglas, Grant, Mason, Lewis, Cowlitz, Pacific and Grays Harbor. It seemed the "furni-

ture" was now being burned to keep the house from freezing.

Strange Bedfellows

Lacking any other prospect for additional power supply, McLaughlin joined the PUDs and municipals in lobbying the federal government to build more dams on the Columbia. He proposed a regional hydropower development plan with public/private/BPA/federal participation and maximum home rule. How could he do this? Was he losing his sense of direction, joining his enemies? Those were the questions then being asked by national business and utility leaders who had previously saluted him as the champion of free enterprise. And

An electric trolley streetcleaner sports an ad for gas in the '20s but in the lean '40s, gas systems were among the first subsidiary companies sold by Puget Power.

Courtesy of the U of W Libraries

Above: The North Coast Transportation Company, which in 1930 took pride in this luxury liner.

Below: The wave of the future: The Greyhound Corporation was destined to absorb Puget Power's last remaining transit holding.

Courtesy of the Museum of History & Industry

these same people were really shaken by his next move.

Facing the threat of an order, reportedly soon to be signed by President Truman, terminating the Rock Island Dam permit, McLaughlin entered into a "marriage of convenience" with the Chelan County PUD. The PUD agreed to finance the federally mandated Rock Island additions. That financing was made possible by a Puget Power contract to purchase a major share of the power generated for 50 years. This was a new and very creative concept devised by Executive Vice President Larry Karrer to provide Puget Power an increment of power supply on the same basis as a like increment would cost the PUD. It was a technique that would be used to finance several other PUD dams on the Columbia River in future years.

By 1949 new fuel had been added to the dozen or more PUD condemnation efforts. The most vigorously pursued was the one by Snohomish County, jeopardizing 12 percent of the company's revenues and 15 percent of its customers. Frank McLaughlin continued to blast both the unfairness of this government-sponsored competitive threat, and particularly the folly of any effort to break up the company's power supply and transmission network county by county. By the end of 1949, in contradiction to McLaughlin's

Larry Karrer, Executive Vice President of Puget Power (seated), masterminded the company's power purchase contracts with mid-Columbia PUDs, still an important power supply resource for the company. With Karrer is George Westerland, assistant treasurer, Central Division.

The familiar axe of public condemnation was turned toward a nervous Reddy Kilowatt in this 1941 anti-take-over display in the company's Bellingham office.

"all or nothing" speeches, the Board of Directors approved the sale of the distribution system in Snohomish County and on Camano Island to Snohomish County PUD. The PUD paid $16.5 million and dropped its condemnation lawsuit. With a weakening cash and credit position, McLaughlin saw no other choice.

To appreciate the bleakness of the company's position, one must remember that this running fire-fight with the PUDs was taking place simultaneously with the debilitating struggle with Seattle City Light (described in the previous chapter). And if McLaughlin's manuevering tactics consternated other industry leaders across the nation, they spurred his counterpart in Spokane to action.

McLaughlin and Robinson

Kinsey Robinson, President of Washington Water Power Company, headquartered in Spokane, was very different from Frank McLaughlin, though the two shared some common elements of background and philosophy. Nearly the same age, both had "bootstrapped" themselves up the ladder from very modest beginnings. While still a teenager, Robinson had gone to work as a groundman/helper for a small utility in Idaho. By age 19 he was a line crew foreman. A fall from a pole caused permanent injury to one leg changing his career direction but not his progress. Moving to sales and administrative jobs he rose to the

98

Kinsey Robinson,
president of
Washington
Water Power.
Courtesy of
Washington
Water Power

presidency of Idaho Power Company in 1934 at age 38, and to the presidency of Washington Water Power in 1938. Both utilities were then owned by American Power & Light Company, a holding company subsidiary of EBASCO [see Chapter 8].

Both men had strong leadership qualities and shared a belief in the merits of investor ownership. Both

Frank McLaughlin,
president of Puget
Sound Power &
Light Company.

were outstanding public speakers. At close quarters however, they were not at all alike, Robinson outgoing and gregarious, McLaughlin reclusive and stern. They never enjoyed each other's company.

The public power takeover struggle had hurt the interests of both Puget Power and Washington Water Power. However, the impact of the municipal system formations and the potential impact of PUD condemnations fell rather more heavily on Puget Power. When McLaughlin found it necessary to negotiate the sale to Snohomish County PUD, Robinson thought he was "caving in." And if that bothered him, the next episode infuriated him!

Following Puget Power's sale of its Seattle properties, six county PUDs — Chelan, Kitsap, Jefferson, Skagit, Snohomish, and Thurston — offered on September 10, 1952 to pay $89,490,000 for all of the company's remaining properties except those in Whatcom County. The Whatcom County PUD had earlier withdrawn from efforts to structure this joint offer. The capacity of county PUDs to join forces in such an offer had been subjected to question and litigation for several years. The state legislature had finally authorized such combinations in a 1949 Act, which the State Supreme Court upheld on February 23, 1951.

The Puget Power Board of Directors considered the six PUDs', offer fair and called a special stockholder meeting to authorize the sale. On October 27, 1952, 84 percent of the common stock shares were voted in favor, two percent opposed. On November 6, 1952 McLaughlin signed a purchase agreement calling for final closing on February 27, 1953. Guy Myers and his correspondent investment bankers would have the intervening 112 days to raise the purchase money. Myers went to work.

So did Kinsey Robinson! He was both terrified and furious. Only in midsummer of that same year, 1952, Washington Water Power had gained its "freedom" from the EBASCO holding company, just as Puget Power had from Stone & Webster in 1943. If Puget Power went down the chute to PUDs, could Washington Water Power be far behind? Why wasn't McLaughlin fighting it out county by county, courtroom by courtroom?

Robinson launched a multi-pronged attack, in effect opening up one more front on the takeover battlefield. He structured an offer to merge the two companies through an exchange of a combination of cash and stock for stock. First discussed in October 1952, and improved in January 1953, the proposition was the basis of an "understanding" between Boards of Directors on March 13, 1953. Meantime, Robinson lent whatever assistance he could to the considerable number of western Washington people trying to stop the sale of Puget Power to the six PUDs. The stipulated closing date for that sale, February 27, 1953, was extended to July 31, 1953 when a combination of factors, including the distraction of Korean War-related activities, impeded the completion of financing for the six PUDs.

As the days of late 1952 and early 1953 came and went, the multi-front battle rose to a fever-pitch. It whirled through courtrooms — PUDs vs.

Municipals, PUD Commissioners vs. their fellow commissioners, PUDs vs. PUDs, PUDs vs. Water Power, Puget Power vs. Water Power, Water Power vs. Puget Power — a lawyer's field day. The merger proposal required the approval of the Public Service Utility Commission, which was somewhat hesitantly given after bitterly contested summer-long hearings.

From the Ashes

The PUDs, which had learned to hate Puget Power, now found something they disliked even more: the single statewide utility that the merger would create. Many Puget Power customers also disliked the merger idea when they realized it meant Puget Power's becoming simply the western division of a Spokane-headquartered utility.

By autumn of 1953 some new perspectives began to emerge. It became clear that the litigation piled on court dockets would require years to clear and meantime would prevent the financing and closing of either the six-PUD purchase or the Washington Water Power merger. Second, the merger hearings before the state Public Service Commission had called attention to the fact that during the past 20-odd years when Puget Power had been unable to finance any major new construction, it had continued payments on its debts. The result was a very strong balance-sheet ratio of assets to debts. If it were freed of the litigation impeding its ability to finance,

Carroll W. Nahrs Loren H. Holden Al Bullock Harold Bishop Irving M. Zeller William H. Deeridan

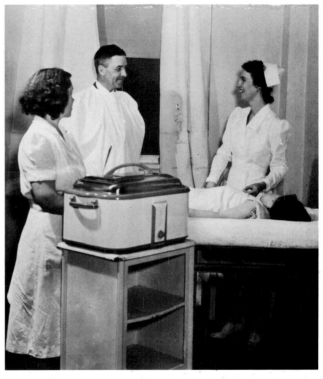

Near left: The company became a more involved supporter of community activities and causes.

Under McLaughlin, Puget Power became increasingly service-oriented. **Far left**: A 105-foot pole was installed in Auburn in 1956 to provide extra clearance at a highway intersection.

Left: Puget Power provided eight Mobile Emergency First Aid units to its Western Division service territory in 1940. Nearly everyone pictured was an Advanced Red Cross First Aider.

Above: Puget Power found new ways to bring electric technology into the health care field. In this 1944 photo, the company's Gale Blanchard (center) works with Lucille Ross of War Aid (right) and Dorothy M. Brown of Children's Orthopedic Hospital, to develop the use of the electric roaster as a "hot pack" in treating infantile paralysis.

H. A. Eagon   Harold T. Hodgson   C. S. Frederickson   Henry E. Toops   George Strang   Lee O. Thompson   Gen'l H. G. Winsor   Mrs. Ruth Doyle   E. H. Worthen   Oliver W. Hyslop   L. J. Bourke

there was no reason Puget Power could not operate successfully.

Finally, a new public appreciation surfaced for the quality of the Puget Power operation and the dedication of its employees. How had these people continued to perform their tasks day-in, day- (and night-) out, while wondering what utility they might be working for next year or next month, whether they might have to move, or whether they would have jobs at all? No one but those who lived through the experience could answer those questions. The Seattle Post-Intelligencer tried to express this new awareness. On October 1, 1953, after word had leaked out concerning difficulties with the six-PUD purchase financing, the P-I published the accompanying editorial written by Managing Editor Edward T. Stone, under the title *A Lively Corpse.* With respect to the presumed corpse of Puget Power, he asked, "Why should there be a funeral at all?" This editorial was immediately echoed on the pages of nearly every town and city newspaper in western Washington. Several of these papers published parallel articles singling out by name those local Puget Power employees recognized for their valuable community service.

Henry Kruse

Henry R. Kruse, from 1923 to 1964, was involved in sales and management positions in every division of the company. While in the Northeastern Division in Everett, he devised the "Kruse Plan," whereby an appliance repairman would go door-to-door to repair electric appliances at cost. Kruse managed Northern Division, and later Southern Division. He was active in the American Legion and became Post Commander of the King County Post #1 in Seattle and State Commander. His activities also included heading the Thurston County Taxpayers Association of Olympia.

Puget Power's drafting room, Seattle, March, 1955. Pictured, from left: Andy Fuller, John Lord, Reg Bastow, Herb Rundle, Jim Peterson, Ivan Pierson, Fred Dier, Chuck Chaney, Orvil Rose, Verne Bollinger, August Klem.

The government should . . . appreciate the fact that all businesses are so intimately associated and interrelated that an injury to one is an injury to all.

—WILLIAM RANDOLPH HEARST

Seattle Post-Intelligencer

TRUTH—JUSTICE   Seattle, Thursday, October 1, 1953   PUBLIC SERVICE

A Lively Corpse

AMID all the din and clatter over who's to inherit and cut up the corpse of the Puget Sound Power and Light Co., *The Post-Intelligencer* believes it is pertinent to ask at this point:

What corpse and why should there be a funeral at all?

For years there has been a universal assumption that the Puget Sound Power and Light Co. was a dying concern.

On this assumption, the people of Western Washington have been presented two alternatives:

1—A monopoly by merger with the Washington Water Power Co., operating out of Spokane.

2—A monopoly of the Public Utility Districts, operating out of no one knows exactly where, but certainly outside King County, which does not have a Public Utility District but which does have a large consumer interest in Puget Sound's facilities.

The Post-Intelligencer believes the time has come when neither of these alternatives is desirable or mandatory.

It believes that the interests of the people of this area will best be served by the Puget Sound Power and Light Co. remaining in business, as a strongly competitive factor in the Western Washington economy.

* * *

THE PUGET SOUND "CORPSE" has turned out to be a lively one indeed.

During 1953 its earnings per share of common stock will be around $1.80. The book value of the stock is nearly $25 a share or more than double its value of ten years ago when it was divorced from the Engineers Public Service Co. and became an independent corporate entity, beholden to nobody but its own stockholders and the people of the Puget Sound region it serves.

At the end of 1952 its property and assets were valued at $111,868,076, only 13 million dollars less than in 1943, despite sales of property amounting to 48 million dollars.

It has required no new financing in 1953.

It has 1,600 employees with an annual payroll of more than 8 million dollars.

With prime power to be available from its expanded Rock Island project after July, 1955, it will be in an advantageous position from the standpoint of power supply.

* * *

WHY THE RUSH, then, to kill off a healthy and growing business which has been part and parcel of this region's industrial structure for many years?

In all the welter of words which have been poured into the records of hearing after hearing, and court action after court action, there has been remarkably little complaint about Puget Sound's service or its rates which, of course, are rigidly regulated by the State Public Service Commission.

The Public Utility Districts take the position that they can give better and cheaper service if they are given the whole works.

But they have not made a convincing demonstration so far of their ability to do so in the counties where they already have exclusive sway.

The Washington Water Power Co. claims it can effect substantial savings by a merger that would be reflected in cheaper or better service. But this is a matter of dispute and the people of this area hardly look with favor on removal of executive and engineering headquarters of their power services to Eastern Washington.

With Puget Sound remaining in business, the element of competition, which is the lifeblood of the American way of life, is retained in full effect. Puget Sound must compete with the Public Utility Districts already operating and with the municipal power systems of Seattle and Tacoma. They do not compete in the same areas, of course, but by comparison of rates and services in the respective counties and municipalities which each serves.

* * *

THERE IS considerable question whether the sponsors of the State Public Power Act, under which the Public Utility Districts came into being, ever contemplated a statewide power monopoly, either privately or publicly owned. There is no question that the reckless practices of private promoters during that period, in which holding company was piled on holding company until it was difficult to determine the actual ownership of an operating utility, brought about a popular demand for proper restraints.

Many people voted for the Public Power Act with the understanding that it was to be used as a curb, through constant threat of condemnation, against any practices contrary to the public welfare.

That curb is in full effect today. The reckless conditions prevailing when the act was first passed no longer exist. Puget is an independent company, closely checked in every conceivable way by state law and regulation.

The Post-Intelligencer believes there is no popular demand for its absorption by either the Washington Water Power Co. or the Public Utility Districts. While we have no quarrel with the laudable desire of Mr. Guy C. Myers, the principal promoter of the PUD purchase plan, to turn an honest dollar for himself, or with that of Mr. Kinsey Robinson of Washington Water Power to extend his company's holdings, we do not believe their interests necessarily coincide with the public interests.

Why not let the people themselves decide?

That is the American way of doing things.

The Post-Intelligencer's 1953 "lively corpse" editorial was instrumental in snatching Puget Power from a premature burial.

The company response to the question "Why a funeral?" came on November 12, 1953. At a Board of Directors meeting it was decided that, considering the unlikelihood of either the six-PUD purchase or the Washington Water Power merger being consummated in the forseeable future, neither proposition would be given any further consideration. When McLaughlin emerged from the meeting he told the waiting and expectant press, "Puget will remain in business!"

After 23 years of struggle there was at last a day of triumph. Puget Power would survive largely because public opinion wanted it to — a welcome message and a powerful lesson!

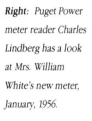

Right: Puget Power meter reader Charles Lindberg has a look at Mrs. William White's new meter, January, 1956.

Far right: Puget Power linemen had to patrol the distribution system by boat during the December, 1946, flood that inundated the Renton-Kent valley. Note the sagging of poles caused by houses, swept away by flood waters, pulling wires with them.

Puget Power's hydro base

Puget Sound Power & Light Company's hydroelectric generating stations at the end of its first century. A strong base of low-cost hydroelectric power has kept Puget Power's rates among the nation's lowest.

Snoqualmie Falls

The Snoqualmie Falls Hydroelectric Plant, located on the Snoqualmie River, consists of Plant No. 1 in a rock cavern about 270 feet directly under the Falls, and Plant No. 2 downstream from the Falls. Four small units were installed in Plant No. 1 in 1898, and a fifth unit was added in 1905. Plant No. 2 with one unit was constructed in 1910. The capability of the project was increased in 1957 by addition of a second unit at Plant No. 2. Net plant capability is 42,000 kilowatts.

Electron

The Electron Hydroelectric Plant is located on the Puyallup River at the town of Electron. A wooden flume ten miles long transports water from the diversion dam to the powerhouse. There are four units, originally installed in 1904. Unit No. 4 was replaced in 1929. Net plant capability is 26,400 kilowatts. The flume has undergone major repairs and rebuild in 1984 and 1985. The flume is topped by an access track regarded as "the crookedest railway in the world."

Nooksack

Nooksack Falls Hydroelectric Project operational since 1906, is on the North Fork of the Nooksack River, about one-half mile below Nooksack Falls, Whatcom County. The river above the project drains 96 square miles, with the source of the river rising in the Mt. Baker area 15 miles from the powerhouse intake. Its single generating unit gives the plant a net capability of 1,700 kilowatts. Power from the project is transmitted by a 55,000-volt line from Nooksack to Bellingham — about 40 miles to the southwest.

White River

This plant is located at Dieringer, between Auburn and Sumner. Water is diverted from White River near Buckley, then flows by a series of flumes and canals into Lake Tapps, the storage reservoir for the plant. Usable storage capacity is 46,655 acre feet. Units No. 1 and 2 were installed in 1912, Unit No. 3 in 1918, and Unit No. 4 in 1924. Generators No. 3 and 4 were rewound in 1952 and 1956, respectively. Net plant capability is 63,800 kilowatts.

Lower Baker

The Lower Baker River Development, built in 1925, is near the town of Concrete, Skagit County, about one-half mile above the mouth of the Baker River. The development consists of a powerhouse and a gravity arch dam 285 feet high, impounding a reservoir, Lake Shannon, with 142,368 acre-feet of usable storage. Two generating units were installed initially; a third was added in 1960 when the Upper Baker River project was built. A landslide destroyed the two older units in 1965; but unit 3 was rehabilitated and enclosed in a "slideproof" powerhouse super-structure in 1969. Net plant capability is 71,400 kilowatts.

Upper Baker

The Upper Baker River Development, about nine miles northeast of Concrete at the head of Lake Shannon, was placed in operation in October 1959. A straight concrete gravity dam and an earth-filled saddle dam back water up a distance of nine miles, creating a reservoir, Baker Lake, having a usable storage capacity of 220,638 acre-feet. The powerhouse contains two units utilizing a maximum gross head of 292 feet. Net plant capability is 103,200 kilowatts.

CHAPTER 11

Here a kilowatt, there a kilowatt

*T*he news that Puget Power would stay in business had some interesting — indeed, surprising — consequences. Both Republican Governor Arthur Langlie and Democratic Senator Warren G. Magnuson hastened to restate their public positions on Puget Power. Langlie, a former mayor of Seattle with a record of political coziness with public power advocates, now said,

> *I am happy that Puget has decided to stay in business ... In view of the many controversies that arose over the proposed merger and the dissatisfactions and problems bound to develop through condemnations, it appears that not only the employees of the Company, but the public generally, would benefit from continuity of management in this area.*

Magnuson, a protege of Senator Bone who owed his election to the violence of his attacks on private power, wrote to McLaughlin,

> *I have come to the conclusion that our real future lies in the development of both private and public power ... I'm sure your decison to stay in business was in response to the real apparent wishes of the people of this region.*

The greatest challenge now facing the

Above: *Reddy Kilowatt tells customers that Puget Power is building for the future, on the site of the rebuild of the Burlington-Dean's Corner 55kv line, 1954.*

Right: *A young Senator Warren G. Magnuson briefs First Lady Eleanor Roosevelt on Northwest issues, 1943.*

Courtesy of the Museum of History & Industry

company (and indeed the region) was the need to catch up in power supply resources. Demand continued to grow. The regional power pooling arrangements mandated during World War II and further refined since, had achieved all of the benefits possible from matching existing resources to differing seasonal and hourly loads.

And though from the standpoint of power supply the company didn't need more load, wonder of wonders: In the closing days of 1953

Puget Power actually purchased four distribution system areas, on Whidbey, Lummi, and Guemes Islands, and an area lost by Seattle City Light when it was annexed by the City of Renton. These were not large acquisitions — total cost $50,000 — but the "corpse" was rising from its premature grave.

The company was now "making up" rapidly for the 60 percent of its business lost to the forced property sales of 1948-51. The story of the company's rapid turnaround from knocking on death's door to "onward and upward" is a dramatic one. Starting from the day in 1943 when freedom from the Stone & Webster holding company and reorganization were accomplished, some severe amputations of service territory had taken place, including Snohomish County and the city of Seattle. However, with each sale of territory, debt had been reduced and operating costs had been cut. Meantime a healthy growth in customers and revenue was taking place in the remaining service area, particularly that part of King County outside Seattle. Even with the twin blades of forced sale and merger hanging over the company's future in 1948-53, the financial base had substantially improved.

In the period 1944-53 the company had averaged an annual return of about 6 percent of the net book cost of its property, regardless of forced sales of properties and the doubling of wage rates, material

costs and taxes. It had increased its earned surplus from nothing to more than $34 million, of which $14 million had come from property sales. The profit on these amounted to $6.46 per share.

The book value of Puget Power's common stock had increased from $10 to $25.66 per share — 160 percent on the original book value, an average of almost 15 percent a year. It had used almost $33 million of proceeds from property sales to reduce 4¼ percent morgage debt about 60 percent. And it had redeemed 137,000 shares of $5 prior preference stock, through a 3 percent term loan, saving almost $300,000 annually in money costs.

Puget Power's common stock had risen in market price from a low of $8.50 per share in 1943 (the

Puget Power's Northern Division Manager John F. Wallin presents a check to Lena M. Ruffalo and C. Clinton Freestone for the electrical properties of Saratoga Light and Water Company, one of two Whidbey Island utilities acquired by the company in April, 1954. At right is Fred Rinehart, local manager of Puget Power's Langley office.

equivalent had been 75 cents in 1933) to almost $29 — 341 percent of the '43 price.

Financial Rebound

Perhaps the most striking evidence of Puget Power's adjustment to adversity is found by comparing revenues from before and after forced sales in the years 1948-1951. The electric properties lost to public agencies had produced a combined gross revenue of about $16 million a year, and were serving 150,000 customers. In 1953, as compared with 1947 (the year preceding the first major sale), operating revenue was down only $6 million or 23 percent. Customers served were but 100,000 fewer than in 1947. Significantly, net income was up about $100,000 (3 percent).

Puget Power's gains were due to new business, and to adjustments of expenses downward, a result of the system contraction consequent to the sales. For instance, Puget Power had 1,527 electric operations employees in 1953, as against 2,594 six years earlier. Many of the displaced workers went onto the payrolls of Seattle City Light and other public agenices that had acquired Puget Power properties.

This residual financial strength did not go unnoticed in New York financial circles. A 1954 survey by Institutional Utility Service, Inc., New York, resulted in this from Charles Tatham, vice president: "For reasons set forth in our report, we believe that the

110

common stock (of Puget Power) has a present reasonable investment value closely centering around $33 per share. Over the longer range considerably higher values can be looked forward to, with a level of around $40 to $46 per share reasonable in prospect within 10 years."

More evidence that the shackles were off came when McLaughlin said that, "Puget is going ahead with area development and aggressive (sales) load building." He added good news for stockholders: "A liberal dividend policy now is entirely appropriate for the company, and will be followed."

Keeping ahead of growth in the number of customers while seeking new industrial load required an aggressive power supply development program. To satisfy the best interests of both customers and stockholders, such a program had to take advantage of the economies of large plants without putting too many company eggs into one generating basket. The answers began to unfold in 1954 when Puget Power obtained a preliminary permit to develop the Upper Baker project.

Partners in Progress

The power supply challenge for investor-owned utilities was doubled by a distinct policy change at the national level. The 1952 election of President Dwight D. Eisenhower had been the turning point, and the change in policy was signaled in

General Dwight D. Eisenhower inspects a Boeing B-50 bomber on a 1947 visit to Seattle.

With the general is A. Elliott Merrill, Boeing Company's project test pilot on the B-50.

his inaugural address:

... The best natural resources program for America will not result from exclusive dependence on Federal bureaucracy. It will involve a partnership of the states and local communities, private citizens and the Federal government all working together. This combined effort will advance the development of the great river valleys of our nation and the power that they can generate.

"Partnership for Progress" was the label generally adopted for this new policy. For the Pacific Northwest the policy was first given meaning by the appointment of new leadership at the Bonneville Power Administration (BPA).

In Northwest power supply terms, the new policy meant no more federally financed dams on the Columbia: less dominance from Washington D.C. — good news! It also meant that as regional electricity consumption grew, the municipal systems and PUDs would, per the "public preference rule," pre-empt the remaining supply from federal dams currently available to investor-owned utilities. Initiating the "partnerships" to solve this new situation was to be left up to local organizations. By way of partial response to this challenge, McLaughlin made Puget Power part of a new organization formed in 1954.

The Puget Sound Utilities Council was composed of Puget Power, Seattle City Light, Tacoma City Light and Snohomish and Chelan County Public Utility Districts — one private company linked to four public-ownership agencies. To many, long inured to the tooth-and-claw relations of the strife-torn electric power industry, it seemed startlingly incongruous. But not to McLaughlin. He saw the new council as "an enlightened and soundly-premised approach to the achievement of adequate low-cost power and the economic growth of the area." He could well understand why such a staid publication as

Business Week should remark, "To anyone who knows the history of power development in the Northwest, it would seem that these five have little in common besides (1) boundaries and (2) a desire to eat each other up."

The new council was given no corporate form. While it was not an operating agency but simply a channel for cooperative effort, it was still intended to be more than a discussion group.

Primarily, the council's resources were to be aimed at its members' problems of power supply; in other words, at the region's power needs. Said the council's first declaration of objectives in 1954: "The five utilities agree it is their responsibility to take care of the total electric power needs of the area for all purposes—including its industrial growth—and they intend to do so." The "declaration" estimated that the region would need 1.6 million kilowatts of additional capacity, to cost more than $500 million "within the next 10 years."

The grand opening of Seattle-Tacoma International Airport, 1948. For 40 years, the airport has remained one of Puget Power's largest customers.

Courtesy of the Museum of History & Industry

The program, purposes and motivation of PSUC at once inspired virtually unanimous acclaim from the region's newspapers. It was apparently an accurate reflection of the public mind. It had been almost 40 years since the power industry had been on the receiving end of so much laudatory and congratulatory comment. For private power in particular, but for public power too, it was a pleasant and heartening experience.

"The basic merit of the Council," McLaughlin said, "rests in the dedication of efforts, previously dissipated in conflict, to cooperative action for the general welfare." It must be hoped that those "efforts" alone provided enough "merit" at the time, for little in the way of concrete results can be found. The solution to power supply requirements would be found through other partnerships.

The Pressure Eases

Of far greater importance to Puget Power's future, the long-menacing threat of condemnation — the key road-block to major financing — began to crumble in 1954. Two Kitsap County PUD actions were dismissed from the courts by agreement, and Sumner's city council instructed its attorney to withdraw a similar action.

The company obtained new 30-year franchises in the cities of Puyallup, Mount Vernon and Sumner, and in the towns of Beaux Arts Village, Everson, Rainier and Tumwater. A 10-year contract to sell 8,000 kilowatts of power was signed with a new Shell Oil refinery in Anacortes. A result of Puget Power's renewed confidence and aggressiveness, the average kilowatt-hour use by residential customers reached an all-time high of 5,854, a gain of more than 12 percent in a year, to a level

The Shell Oil Company refinery at Anacortes added major new load to a recovering Puget Power in 1954.

much above the national average.

As 1955 dawned, McLaughlin forecast that the company would spend $75 million for new construction during the next four years. A year later he would up that figure.

He also was able to announce that, the following Feb. 7, Puget Power would see its common stock admitted to trading on the New York Stock Exchange. First sale: 100 shares to McLaughlin.

By 1955 the axe of condemnation had rusted from disuse. Eight more assaults on Puget Power were with-

Marketing once again, Puget Power continued to promote new uses for the miracle of electricity. The electric lawnmower was a popular item in the increasingly prosperous '50s.

Edith Rauch

*E*dith Rauch, Home Economist from 1925 to 1935 and Home Service Director from 1935 to 1960, was responsible for Puget Power's 10 home service representatives. Their programs consisted of newspaper and appliance-dealer cooking schools where as many as 1,000 people would attend. State fair and high school home economic classes featured the care and use of electric appliances. Puget Power's "Victory Kitchen" at 7th and Olive, Seattle, was also part of the appliance sales program. Edith Rauch was also in demand for radio presentations.

drawn from the courts — 10 now had vanished. The remaining actions — those of the City of Tacoma and Thurston County — affected only 15 percent of company revenues, as against the much higher proportion once threatened.

As the drive now continued to assure Puget Power's power supply, work was started on a $3 million expansion of the Snoqualmie Falls plant, to increase its output from 22,000 to 42,000 kilowatts. Construction work was scheduled for early '56 on the $27 million Upper Baker River development, to provide 110,000 kilowatts, and to make possible expansion of Lower Baker River Dam by 70,000 kilowatts for an additional $8 million.

Puget Power next sold its remaining interest in the Rock Island Dam to Chelan PUD for $28,276,000. The company subsequently negotiated two long-term power contracts with Chelan Public Utility District. One pact covered the Rocky Reach project on the Columbia. Rocky Reach, it was planned, would have initially 644,000 kilowatts of capacity, and ultimately one million kilowatts. The deal also would make available to Puget Power for a period of 48 years not less than 124,500 kilowatts of low-cost Rock Island power—a figure 40,000 kilowatts, or about 50 percent, more than the 85,000 kw capability of the company's facilities at Rock Island taken over by Chelan PUD. What it all added up to was that Puget Power would receive not

less than about half of the power from both Rocky Reach and Rock Island — a total of 426,500 kilowatts — at an attractive rate. Not only had great strides been taken to ensure the company's future power supply, but the $28 million check from Chelan PUD further strengthened the company's financial position. In truth, the company that had pioneered the conquest of Columbia's rushing waters a quarter century before was back on the great river in a big and significant way.

The Building Boom

Puget Power's service area was welcoming a surprisingly large influx of new people. As a result, McLaughlin presented the Board with a 1956 construction budget of about $20 million — double 1955's, and the biggest in 25 years. In addition to much transmission and distribution system expansion, he asked for new Puget Power buildings at Renton and Kirkland and a new headquarters building in Bellevue. All these were fast growing communities in the heartland of Puget Power's suburban electric service empire.

The need for expanded offices and operating headquarters had been identified by rank-and-file employees, supervisors and managers from all across the company. Under the pressure of increased business, the "make-do" mode that had been mandatory for so many years was reaching its limit. The final impetus for these new office

Above: Surveyors take readings for construction of the Upper Baker hydroelectric project, September, 1955.

Below: Construction of Snoqualmie Plant No. 2's second unit, underway in 1956.

buildings, however, came from an outside source. In 1954 McLaughlin had decided that rebuilding the company required the help of outside consulting specialists. He brought in the nationally respected firm of Booz, Allen & Hamilton from Chicago. The company's working relationship with this firm continued for several years and covered such aspects as organizational structure, executive personnel selection, and improvement of tooling, equipment and work procedures in the field. But one of their first recommendations to be implemented was to get on with the new office structures now budgeted.

Puget Power's Bellevue Local Office, at 10507 Main Street, May, 1954.

In the final weeks of 1955, another of Puget Power's problems from the "dark days" was finally resolved. The effort to force a merger of Puget Power with Washington Water Power, which had flared up in 1952 and fizzled out in 1953, suddenly came to life again. The same old group from the New York financial community launched a campaign of mailings urging Puget Power stockholders to join an effort to remove McLaughlin. At a stockholders' meeting in late 1955, with 88 percent of the shares represented, the vote was 99.994 percent in favor of McLaughlin and the existing Board of Directors: end of that struggle.

The effort to build a portfolio of generating resources continued in 1956. During the summer of that year the company concluded a 50-year contract with Grant County PUD to buy at cost 8 percent (approximately 50,000 kilowatts) of the output of the new Priest Rapids power plant on the Columbia, scheduled to be operative in 1959 and to be completed in 1961. The contract also reserved for Puget Power, if wanted, a similar share of production of the projected Wanapum

plant — a short distance upriver from Priest Rapids — which would be constructed in the 1960s. And once again the financing tools used were those pioneered by Puget Power in the first Rock Island transaction with Chelan County PUD. In this case Grant County PUD sold its revenue bonds, backed by the credit of 12 purchasers, in the form of long-term contracts. Four of the purchasers were investor-owned utilities. A similar transaction with Douglas County would later provide Puget Power a one-third share of the output of Wells Dam power for 50 years.

The company was spending more than ever on plant and expansion to care for new business. Line extensions for new customers went in by the hundreds; work went on at Baker River and Snoqualmie; and everywhere in Puget Power's territory buildings were being enlarged, renovated or replaced to better meet service demands.

The King's New Castle

Two weeks before Christmas in 1956, Puget Power formally opened its handsome new General Office Building in Bellevue. The event was symbolic of the company's new look.

Bellevue was then a burgeoning post-war suburb. On the Cascades side of Lake Washington, connected with Seattle by the world-famous Mercer Island "Floating Bridge," it was the heartland of Puget Power's operational area. Just the year before

Right: The first Lake Washington "Floating Bridge" from Seattle to Mercer Island was a sensation when it opened in July, 1940.

Photo by Asahel Curtis Courtesy of the Washington State Historical Society

Below: The Seattle Electric Building, at 8th and Olive, occupied by Seattle Electric Co. in the first decade of the century ...

Left: ... was head-quarters for Puget Power, until the loss of Seattle meant building the company a new home in Bellevue.

Bellevue had been adjudged an "All-American City" in national competition. Bellevue and the remainder of the company's King County service area had doubled in population in 15 years.

The event was declared "Puget Power Day" by the Bellevue Chamber of Commerce. Appropriately, McLaughlin was principal speaker. Gazing at the new building, he called it a "stately and imposing landmark," which indeed it was. "But, after all," he continued, "a building is only a structure. Of far greater import is that here for us is a 'Cathedral of Service' — built on the faith, understanding and confidence of many people and dedicated to the best in fulfilling certain human needs." Once more McLaughlin had

found an opportunity to tell his parable of the cathedral. Some thought it "corny," some referred to it irreverently as "Mac's Mass." But undoubtedly, so far as Puget Power's president was concerned, it was an expression of faith and something closely akin to prayer. Later in the same speech he summarized the basic operating objectives that still survive today:

To successfully fulfill our obligations means that:

The people we serve should obtain courteous, prompt, reliable and efficient service at lowest possible cost;

Those who put their money in the enterprise should receive a fair return on their investment;

We should have employees who are fairly compensated for the work they do, who have the necessary technical skill, who are in complete sympathy with our ideals of public service, who are good citizens and whom you will be delighted to have as neighbors and friends.

Corporations are essentially economic-action institutions in our society.

They must venture and they must risk in order to produce. But in this operation, corporations must take care to recognize the rights of others they do business with. This means that while recognizing the right to bargain with labor, corporations must also recognize

Puget Power's new General Office Building in Bellevue, under construction in early 1956.

117

labor's right to bargain with management. While realizing that a balance must be obtained between industrial and agricultural prices, they must also recognize the right of farmers to a fair return. And while recognizing that consumers should pay a price which yields a fair profit to the corporation, the company must bend every effort to make sure it maintains prices at the lowest possible level.

The favorable trend continued through 1957-58. Thurston County PUD formally dropped its eight-year-old effort to take over Puget Power's distribution system in that county as well as the Electron generating station. Puget Power made one more sale — "under pressure" — of distribution properties in the area of Pierce County competitive with Tacoma City Light for $560,000. In return Tacoma dropped its condemnation actions aimed at all other Puget Power properties in Pierce County, including the generating stations.

During 1957 Puget Power was granted 20 state and county and four municipality franchises. The company spent close to $29 million for plant additions (the most in any year up to then), much of which went to continue construction on Baker River, and to complete (in July) the 22,000-kilowatt enlargement of its Snoqualmie Falls hydro station. Sparkling new service buildings were completed at Puyallup and Burlington; two more were under construction at Factoria and Poulsbo. Several new long-term power sale contracts were signed, the largest with Texaco for up to 12,500 kilowatts for its new Anacortes refinery, to open in 1958.

In 1958 construction expenditures increased to another all-time peak — $33 million. Baker River plant construction was at its height.

The Boss Steps Down

The life of a corporation is a product and a reflection of the collective lives of the individuals who make it move. In 1959 the winds of change were signaling one of those inevitable progress points in the life of Frank McLaughlin. He was now 64 years old. His health was deteriorating, and he was showing understandable signs of "burn-out." He had stood at the helm for over 28 of the company's 74 years, a feat unlikely ever to be repeated. His autocratic style, always a strain on close associates, now became an impediment

Left: The Upper Baker hydroelectric project under construction in 1958.

Right: U.S. Congressman Jack Westland (center) inspects the Upper Baker plant

construction site, accompanied by Norman McKenney, superintendent of construction, Stone & Webster, (left); and Andy Miller, superintendent of Puget Power's Lower Baker plant. January, 1958.

to daily activities. The Board of
Directors insisted that he accept a
reduction in responsibilities and on
September 18, 1959 elected him
Chairman of the Board, a post he
would hold only until January 24,
1960, his 65th birthday.

To many, Frank McLaughlin was
indeed the "white knight" of his
own self-image
— the genius
who fashioned a
Machiavellian
masterpiece in
maneuvering his
archenemies,
the PUDs and
Washington
Water Power
Company, into
mutual frustra-
tion. To others
he was a utility
company leader
with a flair for
publicity, both
the victim and
the beneficiary
of events largely
beyond his control. From any point
of view he must be given this: For
more years than most people count
in an entire career, he stood as head
of Puget Power in the center of a
titanic struggle of political and
financial interests. There must
have been days or weeks or months
when all his human instincts told
him to "chuck it," "pack-it-in,"
bail out."

Frank McLaughlin saw it through.

McLaughlin with pipe
presides over the flag-
raising in front of the
newly-completed
General Office in
Bellevue, 1956. With
McLaughlin, from left:
Eldon C. Wilen, con-
struction and building
supervisor; C. Norman
Dickison, mayor of
Bellevue; E.M. "Buck"
Biddle, a Seattle-First
National Bank manager
and president of the
Bellevue Chamber of
Commerce; and Sam
Boddy, Jr., who chaired
the Puget Power Day
luncheon for the
Bellevue Chamber
of Commerce.

Above: J.H. "Jack Clawson"

Left: In 1960, Puget Power spearheaded the Gold Medallion all-electric home campaign throughout its service territory, seeking to build load and compete aggressively with fuel oil *and gas vendors. Bellevue's Somerset neighborhood was a center of all-electric home-building activity.*

CHAPTER 12

Turning points

For Puget Power the 1960s and 1970s were a time of both continued growth and significant change. The growth was measured in terms of numbers of customers, per capita use of electricty, system load, and consequently in all of the quantities of people, equipment and capital required to deliver service. The change was a function of that growth; but even more of events in the drama of regional and national energy politics. New strategies and management styles were needed to lead the company through a series of critical turning points.

Clawson

J.H. "Jack" Clawson was elected by the Board of Directors to succeed Frank McLaughlin as President of Puget Power on September 18, 1959. Clawson, at age 60, was five years younger than McLaughlin but had longer service with the company, having joined Puget Power in 1927.

His education and experience prepared him well for the job of president. After receiving a bachelor of science degree from Utah State University in 1920, he went on to earn a master's degree in business administration at Harvard in 1922. After graduation, Clawson joined Stone & Webster in Boston, working as an auditor until 1927 when he moved west to Puget Power. His career at the company included the jobs of auditor, assistant treasurer, controller, treasurer (in 1947), and senior vice president (in May 1959, just before becoming president). A man of strong principles, he had a congenial manner of communicating with the departments he had led. He now extended that atmosphere to the entire management team.

One of Clawson's early moves was to initiate in 1960 the reincorporation of Puget Power under a Washington State charter. (The young lawyer the company's law firm assigned to the reincorporation task was John W. Ellis, on his first assignment for the company he would later lead.) Since the 1912 incorporation of the Puget Sound Traction, Light and Power Company in Massachusetts, the company had taken several steps to change its early identity as an eastern firm. This final act, motivated by several considerations, now completed the nearly 50-year move. As a Washington

corporation, the company would now hold its stockholder meetings in the area where most of its stockholders lived.

A general rate increase was granted by the Washington Utilities and Transportation Commission in 1960. This 10 percent increase, the first rate increase in the company's history, was the signal of a new truth: For the first time in 75 years, costs were rising faster than could be offset by the building of newer and larger generating stations.

For many years Puget Power had been disposing of non-electric utility subsidiary operations. In 1960 that trend was reversed with the formation of Puget Western, Inc. This company, and a later parallel subsidiary, Puget Properties, Inc., were established to develop and market some of Puget Power's well-located non-utility real estate. These

Below: Puget Power's Board of Directors: (clockwise from lower left) F.J. Herb, Puget Sound Pulp & Timber Company; Frank McLaughlin; Roy E. Campbell, Arden Farms; Lowell P. Mickelwait, attorney; J.H. Clawson; Joshua Green, Peoples National Bank of Washington; D.K. MacDonald, D.K. MacDonald & Company; Ralph Stormans, Associated Supermarkets, Associated Grocers; Darrah Corbet, Smith Cannery Machines Company.

John W. Ellis, attorney, in the '60s.

subsidiaries were subsequently merged as Puget Western, Inc. One of its holdings — Andover Park in Tukwila — became part of the region's first and largest shopping-mall and business park combination.

In 1964 a Puget Western residential subdivision in Renton was used as a test location for new design concepts in the construction of underground power and telephone service. In addition to developing new field-installation techniques, Puget Power worked with the Federal Housing Administration to obtain recognition of appropriate increases in the value of homes so served, an essential part of system financing. Once again Puget Power demonstrated the ability and willingness to pioneer an improvement in the quality of electric service.

Above: Breaking ground for Puget Western's Andover Industrial Park in Tukwila: Charles O. Baker, Mayor of Tukwila; Clawson; Wells B. McCurdy; Frederick W. Kimball.

Courtesy of the Museum of History & Industry

Right: Andover Park's neighbor, Southcenter Mall — an important development and a major customer for Puget Power.

Underground electrical service was an aesthetic selling point in new housing development during the '60s. Here Puget Power serviceman Bob Burton chats with a young resident of Bellevue's Conifer Crest, one of the first total-underground developments in the company's service area.

Above: Ralph M. Davis

Right: Planning the electric exhibit at Century 21, the world's fair hosted by Seattle in 1962: A.B. Couch, *residential sales director, Bellevue, and H.P. Forman, vice president, public relations.*

The Davis Years

As in 1931, a relatively sudden change in company leadership had again been found necessary in 1959. The Board of Directors now wished to accomplish a more gradual transition in advance of Clawson's mandatory retirement at age 65. Therefore, on June 12, 1962, Clawson was elevated to the position of Chairman of the Board and Chief Executive Officer, and Ralph M. Davis was elected President.

Davis brought to the job a training and experience particularly suited to the challenges of the '60s. Following distinguished service as a combat pilot and administrative officer in World War II, he completed college at the University of Washington, earning a degree in law in 1948. After a brief private practice of law in Bellingham, he became involved in state government, serving in succession as Assistant Attorney General, legislative counsel to the Governor, and, from 1955 to 1957, Chairman of the Washington Public Service Commission. He joined Puget Power in 1957, and by 1962 had been Corporate Secretary and Vice President. He was the first company president in 48 years who owed neither training nor allegiance to Stone & Webster.

The old threats of municipal takeover and PUD condemnation periodically returned to centerstage in the concerns of every employee. In 1960 the "old guard" at Seattle City Light made one more jab —

attempting to extend their service into the Kent Valley. In 1962 Thurston County PUD launched an unsuccessful attempt to build the political base for another condemnation action. Though neither of these efforts approached the magnitude of the 1952 threat, they again demonstrated the need for constant vigilance in maintaining good customer relations. Some longer-term assistance was obtained in 1969 when the state legislature acted to require that a PUD first obtain a favorable vote of its county citizens before initiating the sale and distribution of electricty.

Certainly the major turning point(s) of the 1960-75 period related to the fundamentals of power supply. When the Snoqualmie Falls hydro power plant was first being built in 1898, skeptics had questioned its financial feasibility, since "its output would obviously cover any conceivable demand for 50 years or more." Now over 60 years later, nearly every major river in the Pacific Northwest had been tapped to provide additional electric power supply. That part of the Columbia River within Washington State had been developed to the extent that the foot of each of its eleven major dams stood on the edge of a lake backed up from the next downstream dam. And yet, despite all of that capacity, the challenge was how to keep up with the growth in demand that was nearly doubling

Above: *The drive-in cashier window — another Puget Power customer service innovation. Puyallup Local Office, 1963.*

Left: *Life in a Gold Medallion home: Kay Ruble pours a cup of coffee for her mother, Mrs. E.D. Ruble, a Mercer Island all-electric home equipped with a custom-built oven and hot plate.*

every ten years. Where would we turn for additional supply?

The question had region-wide impact on all electric utilities, regardless of ownership, and had been under study from well before the beginning of the 1960s. The first answer finalized in 1964, required widening the circle of concerned participants to include governments and companies from northern British Columbia to southern California, from Washington state to Washington, D.C. and Ottawa, Canada.

The Canadian Connection

Looking at the vast lakes behind each of the mammoth dams on the Columbia, it's hard to realize that at full generating capacity these "ponds" contain only a very few days of "stored energy." Were it not for the storage provided by Coulee, Coeur d'Alene, and Flathead Lakes, many of the Columbia River generating stations would have been only a little better than "run-of-river" plants. Conversely, during periods of low demand and high runoff, a great deal of water was necessarily being spilled — lost forever as a source of electricity. Capturing that extra runoff was a very attractive goal. The source of the Columbia lies in the mountainous regions of eastern British Columbia where typically heavy snow packs provide large energy storage. Nature's schedule for summer release of this storage does not coincide with the major part of man's need for electricity in the

128

Submarine cables

Puget Power is one of the few electric utilities whose service area is broken up by numerous waterways. Early in the formation of Puget Power's electrical system, it became evident that submarine cables were needed to transmit electricity across these water barriers. A large share of those cables were installed in the 1920s and the early '30s. To lay the cables, Puget Power had constructed a special cable ship, the *Wm. Nottingham.* This ship was

later replaced by a converted Navy barge renamed *The Puget Power.*

The early submarine cables used by Puget Power were rated at 15 KV. All three phases were contained in a rubber-insulated single cable. This type of cable was installed at two cross-sound locations in the late 1920s. One crossing was between Des Moines and Vashon Island. Another was between Richmond Beach, north of Seattle, to President's Point, south of Kingston. Other early cable installations were: Hood Canal Crossing (now adjacent the floating bridge)

The Wm. Nottingham, a former four-masted wood-hull schooner, *was reconditioned for use in laying electrical cable across Puget* *Sound in 1927. The vessel accommodated 22 men and completed* *a trans-Sound cable-laying job in two to seven days.*

Kennydale to south Mercer Island, Enatai to north Mercer Island, Port Orchard to Bremerton, and Bainbridge Island to Bremerton. A cable was later laid between Anacortes and Guemes Island.

In the early 1960s it became obvious Puget Power needed a stronger electrical tie to the Kitsap Peninsula. The load was growing, and a large block of power from the Columbia River needed to be delivered to various points in the company. BPA was about to increase the cost of wheeling power to Western Division. It was decided that it was more economically feasible to install a new and larger cross-sound cable than to rely solely on BPA. The decision centered on laying an oil-filled submarine cable rated at 115 KV between Des Moines and Vashon

Island — a distance of approximately 14,000 feet. A shorter section of 6,000 feet was to be installed between the west shore of the island and the Kitsap shore. This installation at the time set a world record for length and depth, which reached 800 feet at its deepest. The Okanite Cable Company was selected to manufacture the cable at a cost of over $1 million. (The total project cost was in the $2 million range.) Okanite also supplied the engineers to assist in the cable laying.

The first cable laid was the shorter 6,000-foot section and was somewhat routine. The laying of the longer section became a nightmare when insufficient tension was placed on the cables as they were played out, resulting in numerous twisted kinks. All four cables needed to be picked up and salvaged by splicing the good

sections together. The repaired cable was relaid, and the system was placed in service a few months later.

In the 1962 cross-Sound cable-laying operation, (above) workmen attach the lifting rig to move the cable reel from a flatcar to the barge shown in the picture below. Four cables were laid simultaneously as three tugs moved the barge sideways across the sound from Cove, on Vashon Island, to Command Point on the Olympic Peninsula.

Northwest. The answer was a series of storage dams in British Columbia.

A strategy to carry out that plan called for storage dams to be built at Arrow Lakes, Duncan Lake and Mica Creek in British Columbia. The 1964 plan also provided for the building of Libby Dam on a Columbia tributary in Montana, since that project would also impound water on the Kootenay River in British Columbia. The project was attractive to Canada on a long-range basis, though British Columbia had no near-term need for its share of the resulting additional output. As a matter of fact, the additional electricity thus produced would at times exceed the needs of the Pacific Northwest utilities, but would be saleable in California — if only there were a means of delivering it. The ingredients of a four-way agreement to carry out the plan were already in hand.

The physical size of this multi-unit project seemed surpassed only by the magnitude of the negotiating complications. "Conventions" of engineers, lawyers, financiers, and politicians had met in numerous locations over several years. In 1964 four separate but related agreements were concluded:

- A treaty between the USA and Canada provided permission for construction of the three dams in Canada and the Libby Dam reservoir.
- A Columbia Storage Power Exchange agreement called for Pacific Northwest utilities, inclu-

ding Puget Power, to buy for 30 years Canada's 50 percent share of the additional power produced, and to make advance payments, thereby financing the construction.
- A Pacific Northwest Coordination agreement provided for coordi-

nating the operation of the variously-owned hydro electric dams on the Columbia to make maximum use of the resource.

- United States Public Law 88-552 led to authorization for the construction of the Pacific Northwest-Pacific Southwest high voltage transmission tie network through cooperation of federal, investor-owned, and publicly-owned participants.

The end result of this undertaking was to substantially increase the energy production capacity of Columbia hydropower dams. In economic terms Puget Power's overall cost of firm power from the Columbia River system was reduced by 27 percent. Puget Power had again played a lead role in regional energy development, with major burdens in this case borne by Larry E. Karrer, David H. Knight and John W. Ellis.

The Canadian Treaty "plan" showed recognition of the need to go outside the Pacific Northwest hydro base to keep up with the growth in demand for electricity. But even as that plan was being developed, it was apparent that by the time the storage dams could be completed, critical period reserves would already be below acceptable levels. It was time to turn to other than hydropower sources for the period ahead.

Planning for the New Age

What might at first sound like an engineering problem had much broader implications. True, technology was an important element of the challenge ahead, particularly since Pacific Northwest utilities had

David H. Knight, 1975.

no significant and current experience with large thermal power plants. But, for Puget Power the financial side of the problem was of equal concern.

The recent practice of acquiring additions to power supply by long-term contracts with PUD-owned dams on the Columbia, rather than by building its own generating plants, had been the only solution during the time when the imminent threat of condemnation had impaired the company's ability to finance. Now, however, that practice had left the company without a large capital base from which to lever major financing. In any event, the economic size of new thermal plants had grown to a magnitude that would necessitate the joint participation of several utilities, both investor-and publicly-owned. And that in turn triggered concern for the third, perhaps most critical, dimension of the new challenge: What sort of ownership and management structures would be both acceptable and effective in satisfying the various interests involved?

In 1966 BPA administrator Charles Luce initiated a study of this complex problem. In 1967 BPA formed the Joint Power Planning Council (JPPC) with representation from 180 utilities. Luce acted as chairman. This group produced the Hydro-Thermal Power Program (HTPP) of 1968. The label "Program" was somewhat misleading—"Projection" might have been better — since each company and public agency retained its independence in determining which specific projects it would join or sponsor. Contemplating growing reliance on thermal resources, the region's utilities projected a series of plants and tentative operating dates. The schedule foresaw the installation

of additional turbines at several Columbia hydro projects, and for the construction of two coal-fired plants and 20 nuclear plants — all between 1970 and 1990. Enthusiasm for nuclear units was bolstered by the favorable performance of the first commercial power production at the Hanford "N" reactor in 1966, and by the progress being demonstrated in industry-sponsored test operations.

The first thermal plants completed under joint ownership arrangements were the Centralia Coal Plants 1 & 2, sponsored jointly by Pacific Power & Light and Washington Water Power. Puget Power acquired an interest of 7 percent, its first interest in a

Above: Puget Power acquired an interest in the output of Centralia, a two-unit, coal-fired steam generating plant co-sponsored by Pacific Power & Light and Washington Water Power.

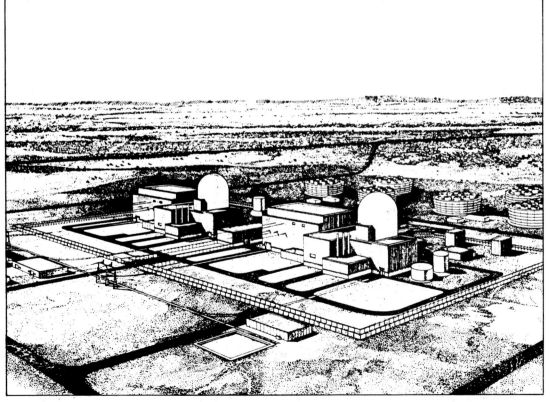

Left: Design for Puget Power's Skagit/Hanford nuclear plant, canceled before construction began.

132

thermal plant since construction of the Shuffleton Plant in 1928. Seattle City Light together with other public agencies acquired a 28 percent share. However, future public agency plans abandoned the joint owner-ship arrangement used at Centralia in favor of joining the Washington Public Power Supply System. Thus, the investor-owned utilites were left essentially to go it on their own. Puget Power proceeded with a plan to participate with other private utilities in the construction of several planned coal and nuclear plants.

The business recession of 1969-70 caused only a temporary setback in the growing development of Puget Power's service territory. The rate of load growth at "double every 10 years" quickly resumed. With responsibility to meet that demand and a desire to spread the location of major generating stations, Puget Power began in 1972 planning the Skagit Nuclear Power Plant slated to be built on Backus Hill adjacent to the Skagit River in the northern part of Puget Power's service terri-tory. Puget Power was to be the lead partner on this project, and to con-trol its construction and operation.

The fortunes of the Puget Sound region suffered a setback during the business recession of the early '70s.

Courtesy of the Seattle Times

Puget Power became a participant in a second nuclear project in 1973: WPPSS Nuclear Project No. 3 was sponsored by a consortium of 19 public utility districts and the cities of Ellensburg, Richland, Seattle and Tacoma, whose acronym "WPPSS" came to be pronounced unflatteringly as "whoops." Puget Power committed to a five percent ownership interest in Project No. 3, which was to be constructed and operated by WPPSS.

Since 1960 Puget Power had navigated several major turning points. But the whirlpools were still ahead.

Above: *Visitors to Century 21 in 1962 stroll around the Pavilion of Electric Power, co-sponsored by Puget Power.*
Right: *The pavilion under construction, just before the opening of* the fair. The fair was credited with boosting interest in the Puget Sound region as a place to live and work — beginning the growth momentum that Puget Power's service area still enjoys today.

CHAPTER 13

Sand in the works – Arab Style

The turn to thermal power sources was not a minor course correction. Almost simultaneously with the start of the Skagit Nuclear Project, Puget Power entered a joint venture with Montana Power Company to build the first two units of a four-unit, mine-mouth, coal-fired generating station at Colstrip, in southeastern Montana. Load growth patterns and growth projections based on best available data indicated clearly that both projects were needed. The four units of the Colstrip project were originally scheduled to come on line in '75, '76, '78 and '79.

Energy and the Environment

A growing national concern for the physical environment led Congress in the late 1960s and early 1970s to pass such laws as the National Environmental Policy Act, the Clean Air Act and the Clean Water Act. Concern for the physical environment was not new to Puget Power. Devising systems to move fish around dams and exercising care in the siting of its lines and substations had long been standard company operating procedures. But the new acts increased

Jerry Kirk, owner of Kirk's Chevron, Bellevue, posts a sign of the times at the height of the energy crisis.

Courtesy of the Seattle Times

Puget Power anticipated and responded to the new environmental consciousness in many ways. The fish trap at Lower Baker stops adult salmon on their upstream spawning journey and holds them for removal and transplant above the dam.

136

by an order of magnitude the detailed requirements and the costs of compliance.

Financing the new thermal projects required the development of new securities and even a new financing subsidiary company. New organizational questions and personnel problems had to be solved. Launching the Skagit project necessitated the addition of many new employees with the required credentials in nuclear technology, many of whom were not familiar with the traditional disciplines of the utility business. And though Montana Power Company was directly managing the Colstrip coal-fired project, Puget Power's interest required that teams of engineers and auditors be routinely air-shuttled back and forth to Colstrip. All this activity had been superimposed on an already high level of day-to-day functions such as serving customers, extending lines,

improving computer-based information systems, and maintaining equipment and facilities.

The Oil Crisis

As new and complex as these challenges were, the company was making progress on all fronts when in 1974 the world, the nation, and Puget Power were struck by one of the greatest economic blows of the century: the Arab Oil Embargo. Inflamed by their losses in Middle East wars, attributed to U.S. support of Israel, the Saudis cut off oil shipments to America. World oil prices skyrocketed to eightfold and more. Utilities heavily dependent on oil-fired generation were hit with suddenly mushrooming fuel costs, followed by large and unpopular emergency customer rate increases. Puget Power had no oil-fired base load generation, but it shared the burden of the rapid inflation that hit

Above: The "fish gulper" on Baker Lake collects young salmon and allows them to bypass the dam and power house, continuing their out-migration downstream.

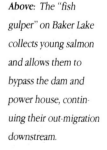

Far left: Lifting adult salmon from the fish trap at Lower Baker for transfer into a waiting "fish taxi" ... *Left:* ... to be released into Baker Lake, above the Upper Baker dam.

the entire economy as nearly all energy prices were bid up. As interest rates began the long rise to record-setting levels, the impact on major long-lead-time construction projects was a serious concern.

Enter John Ellis

The cumulative burden of the major multi-state construction program, newly complex financing requirements, more frequently required rate-case actions, and increased need for inter-company collaboration on common utility problems motivated the Board of Directors to reinforce the manage-

ment structure. On January 29, 1976 Ralph Davis was elected Chairman of the Board, a position from which he could concentrate on important outside contacts, and which he would hold until retirement in 1979. John W. Ellis was elected President and Chief Executive Officer.

Ellis was certainly no newcomer to the problems of an electric utility. After earning a law degree at the University of Washington in 1953, he joined the Seattle law firm of Perkins, Coie, Stone, Olsen & Williams. That firm has been Puget Power's principal legal counsel for many years, and Ellis had become

increasingly involved with this major client. His first job for Puget Power, in 1960, was the legal work transferring its corporate domicile from Massachusetts to the state of Washington [Chapter 12]. As the law firm's partner in charge of the account, Ellis played a key role in the negotiations leading to the 1964 Canadian treaty and related agreements. He had also guided the company's efforts in numerous rate proceedings before the WUTC. Ellis was brought into the Puget Power organization in 1970 as Vice President, Utility Management, and advanced to Executive Vice President

This service station closed at 11:40 a.m. on January 27, 1974, its gasoline allotment already gone for the day.

Courtesy of the Seattle Times

John W. Ellis

in 1973. Always a team builder, he now brought that approach to the growing maze of company challenges.

These challenges differed in many ways from the struggles of the 1940-50 era. This time they were shared in fundamental ways by all Northwest utilities, though the various proposed solutions were no less controversial. Puget Power had undertaken the Skagit and Colstrip projects; other investor-owned and publicly-owned utilities had taken a share of the regional supply requirement in the form of such thermal plants as Pebble Springs and Boardman in Oregon, and Washington Public Power Supply System (WPPSS) plants No. 1, 2, 3, 4 & 5 in Washington.

Regional Challenges, Regional Change

By the second half of the 1970s, interest rates and runaway inflation were driving costs up dramatically, and plant completion schedules were lengthening. Case in point: Colstrip. What a difference a few years made in the '70s! When Units #1 and #2 were announced, Puget Power was welcomed by Montana politicians and public alike. Unemployment was high, and the initiation of a new plant was hailed by one and all. Units #1 and #2 were completed on schedule in 1975 and 1976. But by the time Units #3 and #4 were in the licensing stage, the climate had cooled. The enactment of the Montana State Siting

Act provided a new forum in which opponents of the plants were able to drag out the state licensing process. Colstrip #3 and #4, originally scheduled for completion in 1978 and 1979, saw their completion delayed almost six years, finally coming on line in 1984 and 1986.

In 1976, Puget Power traded part of its interest in its proposed Skagit Project for an interest in the proposed Pebble Springs Nuclear Project being undertaken by Portland General Electric Company in Oregon, ending up with a 40 percent interest in the Skagit Project and a 23.5 percent interest in the Pebble Springs Project.

Licensing proceedings on both the Skagit and the Pebble Springs projects were conducted before state agencies and before the Nuclear Regulatory Commission. Utilities seeking NRC permits had to pre-commit to the specific project design and select the manufacturers of the major components in order to process an NRC license application. This meant that a license applicant not only had to design the project before a license could be obtained but also had to commit to purchase major components of equipment for the project, exposing itself to substantial cancellation charges if necessary permits and licenses were not issued. Applicants for NRC permits and licenses regularly incurred many millions of dollars in costs of nuclear projects before knowing whether they would be

allowed to build anything. Puget Power was no exception. Result: Electric utilities necessarily committed substantial sums of money well in advance of having the licenses in hand to construct and operate a nuclear project.

All the while, demand for electric power continued to grow. The Pacific Northwest was enjoying a brisk economy, and the possibility of electricity shortages loomed larger than ever. BPA was notifying its various customers that it would not have enough power to meet their demand. The delicately balanced institutional arrangements for sharing federal power threatened to

Units 1 and 2 of the spectacular Colstrip coal-fired steam plant in southeastern Montana were finished on schedule in the mid '70s. Units 3 and 4 faced a different picture.

break out into a litigious war among those competing for BPA power.

Efforts toward planning and constructing regional generation had begun in the late '60s [Chapter 12]. They succeeded at first because they were essentially voluntary. By the mid '70s disputes over environmental and siting problems and the resulting delays in licensing threatened to bring the program to a halt. The issues in every licensing proceeding were invariably the same. If a coal plant was proposed, the opponents would suggest substituting a nuclear plant elsewhere; and vice versa. Load projections, the "need for power," were always in dispute. Environmental problems could always be solved by moving elsewhere. Ancient earthquake faults seemed to be uncovered no matter what the location.

Efforts began toward establishing a regional body able to make broad forecasts of needs and thereby produce a "need for power" consensus. The regional body was also expected to be able to help plan the ultimate location of new large-scale generation and, perhaps, aid in reducing finance costs. Based on the initial efforts, Senator Henry M. Jackson introduced in 1977 legislation that led ultimately to the formation of the Pacific Northwest Electric Power and Conservation Planning Council. Before that effort could be implemented however, the entire electric utility industry was dealt a devastating blow.

Computerization

*I*n the fall of 1985 the company's power dispatchers at the Eastside System Operations Center, and system operators in each division, began using the Energy Management System (EMS). Many years in planning and two years in construction and installation, this computerized system places the entire transmission and generation network under the central control of the power dispatchers and system operators.

For many years the power network was controlled by men stationed around the clock at major substations. Phone lines were used to relay information to and from the power dispatchers. Over the years the manned substations have gone through various stages of automation using "hardwired" supervisory equipment that differed for each substation. Calibrating the accuracy of this equipment and maintaining it became more difficult as time passed.

EMS combines all substation and generation plant control units into one comprehensive system. Each substation and generating plant is continually scanned by the computers every few seconds. Power dispatchers and system operators, using cathode ray terminals from the computers, know instantly of changes anywhere

in the network. In addition, EMS controls the amount of power generated for Puget Power customers and stores power accounting information for billing purposes. Every hour EMS takes a "snapshot" of power network information, which is recorded for historical and planning purposes.

EMS has completely changed the way Puget Power operates the power network, and as sophisticated analysis-type software programs are added to this computer system in the future, System Operations will further enhance the service customers have come to know and expect.

Above: Puget Power engineer Pushpakant Patel headed the project that brought the company's generating and transmission network under a computerized Energy Management *System in 1985 ...*

Below: ... a far cry from the days when every substation was adjoined by an operator's cottage, and on-site human supervision was needed 24 hours a day.

TMI and the Crisis of Confidence

On March 28, 1979 a combination of mechanical and personnel failure caused the nation's most serious nuclear power plant accident at General Public Utilities' Three Mile Island Project in Pennsylvania. The follow-on investigations led to a tidal wave of new governmental regulations mandating the redesign and retrofit of commercial nuclear power projects. Public confidence in nuclear power dissolved in hysteria-induced visions of earth-boring melt-downs and torrents of radio-active rain.

This heightened concern, coupled with several other circumstances, sealed the fate of the still unbuilt Pebble Springs and Skagit Projects. Licensing hearings before the NRC concerning the Skagit Project had come to a halt by October, 1979, following the TMI accident. In that year's November election, Skagit County voters opposed the project in an unprecedented advisory ballot. That same month, in view of the advisory ballot, Skagit County refused to extend a temporary rezoning agreement that would have permitted the project to be located at Backus Hill. Puget Power chose to keep its permit application before the NRC active even as opposition mounted, but announced deferral of nuclear construction for two to three years. On July 16, 1980, it announced plans to move the proposed site for the project from Skagit County to the Hanford Nuclear Reservation in south central Washington.

Public sentiment over nuclear generating stations following the Three Mile Island accident was no more favorabe in Oregon than it was in Washington. When Puget Power agreed to participate in the Pebble Springs Project in 1976, that project already had initial approval of the Oregon Energy Facility Siting Council and was well on its way to receiving the necessary federal permits and licenses from the NRC. However, in the November, 1980 general election, Oregon voters

Then...

The control room and mimic board at Puget Power's load dispatching station in the Seattle Electric Building, 1949: a maze of switches, phones, meters and lights. Minute by minute, load dispatchers like Gould Mathis (left) and Scotty Ewart worked to keep Puget Power customers supplied with reliable power and the lowest available cost.

passed Ballot Measure No. 7. This voter initiative conditioned the construction of new nuclear generating projects in Oregon on the existence of an approved federal waste disposal program and on voter approval of the proposed site. Although the initiative had arguable constitutional infirmities, courts had upheld similar laws in other states; and it was this initiative that caused the Pebble Springs participants finally to terminate the project formally on October 8, 1982.

The proposed Skagit project came to the same end a year later. On April 27, 1983, the Regional Council issued its first Regional Power Plan under the Regional Power Act. That plan did not include the Skagit Project as a resource necessary to meet the region's electrical power loads over the ensuing twenty years. Under those circumstances, on October 29, 1983, the Board of Directors instructed Puget Power's management to formalize an agreement with its co-participants to cancel the Skagit Project.

Longstanding principles of public utility law allow utilities to recover through customer rates the costs incurred in discharging their electric service obligations. By the time the Pebble Springs and Skagit Projects were canceled, about 100 other proposed nuclear power plants in the United States had also been can-

The 1979 accident at General Public Utilities' Three Mile Island plant hastened beneficial changes in the nuclear industry, but hurt the public image of nuclear power.

...Now

The technology has changed, but the job remains the same. The mimic board and dispatchers' desks at Eastside System Operations in Redmond shows the changes wrought by the new Energy Management System. Jim Dodge (on ladder) surveys the scene. Craig Lane works in the background as Karen Kelly works with Bill Morton (above) and Dennis Christopherson.

celed by similar pressures. The staggering total investment in these canceled plants brought substantial political pressure to bear on regulatory commissions to depart from the traditional cost-recovery principles under which electric utilities are regulated. Puget Power, upon cancellation of the Pebble Springs and Skagit Projects, became vulnerable to these pressures.

Fortunately, in well-reasoned opinions issued in 1983 and 1984, the Washington Utilities and Transportation Commission resisted the pressure and held that the company should recover the majority of its investment in these two canceled nuclear projects. Applying a balancing-of-interests test, the commission found that such recovery served the long-run interests of both the company and its customers, whose service depended on a financially viable utility.

The Attorney General of the State of Washington and a consumer group appealed the commission's decision, and the issue was eventually resolved by the Washington State Supreme Court in December, 1985, in a favorable opinion that thoroughly examined the legal underpinnings of utility regulation. In upholding the WUTC's decision on rate recovery, the State Supreme Court observed that the commission is "empowered to allow a utility to amortize to expense costs incurred in an abandoned electrical gener-

The accident at TMI catalyzed a mood of resistance to nuclear power nationwide. Here a protester pauses during a walk through downtown Bremerton in April, 1980.

Courtesy of the Seattle Times

These charts show how electric rates have generally declined over the century as the number of customers and amount of electrical consumption has risen. Earliest rates (not shown) were based on the number of lamps of specific sizes rather than on kilowatt hours consumed. The first graph, scaled in both "current" dollars (at the time) and "constant" dollars (1987 equivalents) shows the dramatic decreases up to the mid-'70s, then subsequent increases as thermal power sources were added to a fully developed hydropower base-supply. (Note: KWH = kilowatt hours. GWH = gigawatt hours = one million KW.)

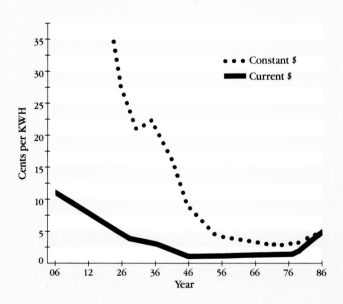

Representative Residential Rates
1906-1986

••• Constant $
▬ Current $

ating project, if the project was prudently undertaken and terminated by the utility."

With the inclusion in rates of Puget Power's investment in the terminated Pebble Springs and Skagit Projects, the company's involvement in nuclear generating facilities was almost at an end. Its only remaining investment in such facilities was the 5 percent ownership interest in WPPSS Project No. 3. Unlike the Pebble Springs and Skagit Projects, Project No. 3 was well under construction before its future became uncertain.

The Fall of WPPSS

The eventual fate of Project No. 3 can be understood only in the context of the broader saga of WPPSS. WPPSS was organized as a municipal corporation in the State of Washington in January 1957, pursuant to specific enabling legislation. As a "joint operating agency," consisting of Washington public agency utilites, it had the authority to acquire, construct and operate generating and transmission facilities. In 1969 WPPSS made ambitious plans to construct three nuclear plants; and then, in 1974, added two additional reactors as "twin" units to two of the three already planned for construction. Twin Project Nos. 1 and 4, and Project No. 2 were to be on the Hanford Reservation. Twin Project Nos. 3 and 5 were to be near Satsop, west of Olympia. Four investor-owned utilities (Pacific Power & Light Company, Puget Sound Power & Light Company, The Washington Water Power Company and Portland General Electric Company) agreed to own and finance ownership shares totaling 30 percent of Project No. 3.

WPPSS financed its portion of Project Nos. 1-3 differently from Project Nos. 4 and 5. Project Nos. 1-3 were "net-billed" to BPA: The power revenues of BPA's power system stood behind the bonds that were issued for those projects. Project Nos. 4 and 5, on the other hand, were financed on the basis of promises by the public agency

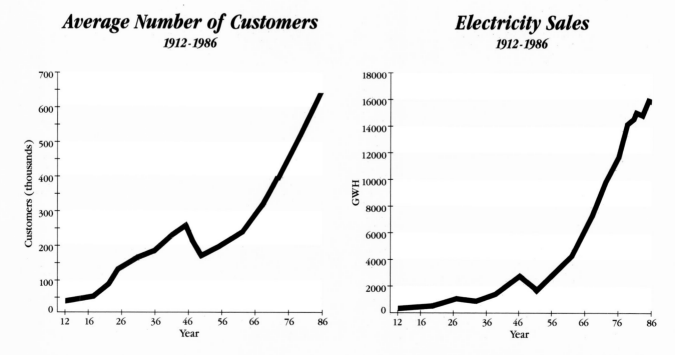

Average Number of Customers
1912-1986

Electricity Sales
1912-1986

participants in those projects to use their system revenues to support the project bonds.

The total cost to build WPPSS' five planned nuclear plants was officially estimated at $6.671 billion, when WPPSS started its long-term borrowing program for those projects. By 1981, when all five projects were actively under construction, that estimate had jumped to $17.327 billion. In addition, the completion dates for each of the projects had slipped on average about five years.

Rumblings over WPPSS' cost overruns and schedule delays caused the Washington State Senate Energy and Utilities Committee to conduct an inquiry entitled "Causes of Cost Overruns and Schedule Delays on the Five WPPSS Nuclear Power Plants." This inquiry resulted in a report to the 47th Legislature in January 1981. The report was highly critical of WPPSS and served to focus the attention of the public and the financial community on the question of WPPSS' ability to finance its ambitious construction program, as well as on the need for the five projects.

The reaction of the financial community to these rumblings was swift. In June 1981, Moody's Investor Services downgraded the ratings on the bonds for Project Nos. 4 and 5, Wertheim & Company advised termination of those projects, and Drexel, Burnham, Lambert, Inc. predicted the projects would be terminated. In July Merrill, Lynch issued a report suggesting that if the public agency participants in Project Nos. 4 and 5 did not issue certain guarantees and make certain rate increase commitments, further debt issuance for completion of construction on those projects was not possible.

Despite efforts by the Governors of Washington and Oregon to effect an orderly suspension of construction on Project Nos. 4 and 5, WPPSS had no choice but to terminate those projects abruptly on January 22, 1982, in view of their financial status. What followed was perhaps the sorriest chapter on municipal finance in the history of this country.

Then...

Beginning in the war years, women assumed a bigger role in the Puget Power workforce. Arlene Hooper, shown here on the job in spring, 1944, was one of the first women to move out of clerical work to become a "meterman."

After termination of Project Nos. 4 and 5, most of the public participants in those projects refused to repay the $2.25 billion in debt that had been borrowed to support construction. In 1983, the Supreme Court of the State of Washington legitimized this refusal by holding, in the case of Chemical Bank vs. WPPSS, that the Washington public agency participants had no authority to commit their electric revenues to support the bonds for these uncompleted generating projects. The result has been heralded as the largest municipal bond default in history — $2.25 billion in principal amount. The resulting allegations and lawsuits implicating various public agencies, officials and professions was inevitable. When and how these suits will be resolved remains uncertain.

The WPPSS debacle had some nasty spill-over. Although Puget Power never was a member of WPPSS or a participant in Project Nos. 4 and 5, WPPSS' general financial condition caused suspension of construction on Project No. 3 in the spring of 1983. At that time, 75 percent of the physical work on the plant had been completed, and it was proceeding on a fast track to full completion by early 1987. BPA, which was responsible for paying the costs of WPPSS' financing under the "net billing" arrangement, was a primary motivator of this construction suspension.

Puget Power and the other three investor-owned utilities owning an interest in Project No. 3 promptly sued both BPA and WPPSS in the summer of 1983 requesting both resumption of construction and damages. Litigation and settlement negotiations progressed among the investor-owned utilities, BPA and WPPSS, and after several preliminary legal victories by the investor-owned utilities, a settlement agreement was worked out which intended to place the investor-owned utilities in the same position they would have been in if the project had been completed. Under the settlement

...Now

The '60s brought increasing educational opportunities for women, and the women's movement of the '70s and '80s caused another dramatic change in workforce composition. At Puget Power today, it's business as usual for meter tester Melody Miller at the company's Renton Meter Shop.

agreement Puget Power received the right to power from BPA in an amount and at a cost meant to approximate what it would have received from its share of Project No. 3 if that project had been completed, adjusted to reflect the fact that Puget Power had only invested approximately two-thirds of what it would have cost to ultimately complete the project. With the consummation of that settlement agreement in September 1985, Puget Power effectively concluded its involvement in the region's ambitious nuclear generation program.

Puget Power and the other investor-owned utilities that held shares in the output of Project No. 3 were never members of WPPSS, and had no responsibility for nor involvement in the cost overruns and the eventual bond default. That fact, however, made no difference to the general public, who did not distinguish between PUDs and municipals on the one hand and investor-owned utilities on the other. All electric utilities, regardless of ownership or affiliation, felt — and continue to feel — the criticism and scrutiny of the public at large as a repercussion of the WPPSS collapse. In the long term, that event may rival the Three Mile Island accident in its impact on the electric industry as a whole, affecting forever the way utilities do business and the way they are perceived by their customers.

Courtesy of the Seattle Times

While public sentiment curtailed nuclear power plant development all across the nation, Puget Power's power supply future lay in a different direction: The company's largest investment to date was in the four-unit, mine-mouth, coal-fired steam generating plant at Colstrip, Montana. A model of environmental harmony, the Colstrip project completely reclaims mined lands in about two years, and has state-of-the-art emission controls.

Better active today than radioactive tomorrow

Colstrip, Montana,
where Puget Power
invested in an
important thermal
generating resource
and helped build a
thriving community.

CHAPTER 14

New realities – the future is now

As the electric utility high drama of the 1970s came to a close, there was a least one favorable turn in Puget Power's path. The Montana litigation that had so long delayed the Colstrip #3 and #4 projects was concluded with a go-ahead. This was a most welcome event after the post-Three Mile Island decline of the nuclear program. Colstrip Units #3 and #4 were subsequently completed in 1984 and 1986. The total capacity of the four-unit project is 2,100,000 kilowatts.

Most interestingly, Puget Power's Colstrip participation gave the company a lesson in civics: The project involved the creation of a brand new town, complete with stores, schools, libraries and recreation centers. Members of the Northern Cheyenne Indian tribe, whose land adjoined the project, were trained in various skills and trades and ultimately participated not only in the construction of the plants, but also in their operation.

Today Colstrip is a flourishing community, an accomplishment that can be viewed with real satisfaction. Equally remarkable, the Colstrip projects, two states away, 740 air miles from Puget Power's Bellevue headquarters, today represent Puget Power's largest single investment.

Important progress on the effort to develop a regional electric power planning mechanism came in 1980 when Congressional legislation authorized the formation of the Northwest Electric Power and

Conservation Planning Council, with representation from the States of Washington, Oregon, Idaho and Montana.

Shortage had been the driving force behind the legislation; but each segment of the industry also had a particular objective of its own. The direct service industries (aluminum manufacturers) sought renewal of their 20-year contracts with BPA. The public agencies wanted BPA to have available additional supplies for their use. Puget Power and the rest of the private companies wanted access to the low-cost federal hydro power for their residential and rural customers.

By the time the Regional Council had prepared its first supply plan, the supply situation had changed dramatically. As a result of a long recession, which included the permanent loss of a number of large industries, and the increasing competition of other fuels as electric prices mounted, load growth slowed and, for many utilities, halted or actually reversed. A council whose founding premise was shortage now presided over a regional surplus. But among the major regional utilities, Puget Power stood out from the crowd. Because of continual growth, it had no excess power supply: The company was (and still is) a net purchaser of energy. The region's surplus provided a ready supply. The dual problems of how to minimize increases in customer rates and how

Above: One of the aims of the Regional Power Act was to provide Puget Power's farm and residential customers with a fair share of low-cost federal power.

Left: Aluminum industries, a mainstay of the Columbia River economy and a large consumer of electric power, have had their interests balanced with the needs of public and investor-owned utilities.

151

"If you're wasting energy and money,

I'm interested in a No-Interest Conservation Loan and would like a free Home Energy Analysis. Please phone me about it.

NAME _____
ADDRESS _____
CITY _____
STATE _____ ZIP _____
PHONE (Home) _____ (Work) _____

Mail to: GENERAL MARKETING DEPARTMENT, Puget Power Building, Bellevue, WA 98009.

cut it out."

to provide for the continuing demand growth (at more modest rates) were at the top of the company's list of challenges. One part of the answer was CONSERVATION.

The Conservation Era

One of Ellis' first acts in joining the company in 1970 as its Vice President Utility Management and Chief Operating Officer, was to give a speech to the Electric League, a group of regional utilities and suppliers. He raised the specter of dramatically increasing rates (at that time Puget Power's average rate was about 1.5 cents per kilowatt hour), predicting that rates would "double, or even triple" in the next decade, as

Then...

In March, 1930, this team of Puget Power meter readers got together to model their newly designed uniforms. From left, front row: G.H. Woodhouse, G.E. Ecklund, L.H. Legas. Back row: A.V. Lorentzen, R.A. Whipple, R.E. Shannon, F.R. Stanton.

thermal additions came into the system. He also described a new program at Puget Power to be called "power conservation" (at that time "conservation" was a popular term, used widely by the environmental community to refer to reforesting practices and resource renewal). The program involved incentives for large industrial customers and all-electric schools to interrupt their loads when requested at daily high-load periods during the winter peak. Although this program was essentially peak-directed, Ellis also predicted that sometime in the future, as kilowatt hours became more expensive and difficult to obtain, it "might even be necessary

to think of an 'energy' conservation program." Little did he know at the time that his prediction would shortly turn into reality.

Two factors combined to make that happen. First, as the potential of a future shortage grew and fuel costs skyrocketed, the need to conserve resources already at hand began to be recognized as a means of filling the gap. And second, as the construction cost of new plants began escalating at unheard-of levels, the burden of financing was overwhelming the financial capabilities of both the utilities and their customers. Conservation provided a means of carrying a portion of the load while ameliorating the impact of increased

rates by reducing customer usage.

At first customer acceptance was sporadic. The early programs assumed customers would make their own investments in conservation improvements in order to realize the future savings in electric bills. It was only when the company began offering interest-free loans — and ultimately paying directly for cost-effective improvements — that the program took off. By year-end 1986, the company had invested a total of $145,000,000 and achieved enough annual savings to power 42,500 homes.

The idea was disarmingly simple: The energy saved would delay or avoid the addition of higher-cost

supplies for which all customers would pay. But simplicity didn't make adoption of the plan easy. A complete reorientation was necessary to prepare long-dedicated company sales people, who had spent their careers selling electricity, to say, "We want to help you use less!" Conservation has now been accepted as a way of life, one of the "new realities." It has been formalized through State Building Codes and the activities of the Regional Council. As a side note, in 1979 when Puget Power's Skagit plant had been effectively stopped by the Three Mile Island incident, and Colstrip #3 and #4 were still tied up in lawsuits, and there

appeared to be no way supplies could be created fast enough to serve future demands, the company found itself proposing what has to be the ultimate conservation program. It asked for and received WUTC approval to refuse to hook up new electric load where other energy sources were available. This particular program ended abruptly when the Superior Court struck it down as unlawful under the state's utility statutes.

Listening

However, despite achievements in conservation (and Puget Power was a leader), and notwithstanding continuing improvements in

productivity, Puget Power rates continued to rise as the cost of its new plants began to be felt. The customer reaction was entirely expectable. During the '60s, led by Ralph Nader, and intensifying in the '70s with environmental acts of various kinds, came the so-called "consumer movement." The movement was essentially based on the theory that the individual should have more to say in activities affecting him, whether they be environmental, financial, or otherwise.

The rise of the consumer movement brought many questions to bear on electric power companies. Should plants be sited in certain

Then...

Puget Power's Western Division office (shown here in 1941) was a downtown Bremerton storefront until 1981 ...

locations? Were rate increases justified? Were people really willing to conserve? No longer were customers content to sit and pay the bill. It was clear that customers were going to be involved in the decisions that affected them, and that one way or another they had to be better informed about those matters, if the utility was to make its case. And the utility had to do a better job of listening to its customers.

Ralph Nader, leading consumer advocate of the '70s.

Courtesy of the Seattle Times

The era of public participation had dawned, and it was up to Puget Power to recognize and react to another "new reality." The company did so in 1980 by forming a series of 13 customer advisory panels throughout its service territory, to which company policies and problems could be referred for review and recommendation. Over 500 panel members were recruited from all political persuasions and from a representative mix of both friends and adversaries. At the time, no other organization in the nation had undertaken a customer involvement program of this scope and magnitude. Councils were asked to consider and recommend alter-

...*Now*

... when a modern office was opened on Sylvan Way, exemplifying the company's contemporary energy-efficiency philosophy.

natives available to the company in matters affecting customer services, power supply resources, billing information, rates and rate structures, and more. The program was initially viewed with skepticism, not only by the public generally, but by a substantial number of company employees. The fear of letting outsiders "run" the business was not easy to dispel.

The program, however, turned out to be an unqualified success and has been continued each year. Puget Power was twice given national recognition for this program, pioneering effort, and many utilities throughout the country now have similar programs. Consumer Panel

Then...

Puget Power employees make beautiful music together. The Puget Power Band in the late '20s (from left): Front row: Frank Ripley, banjo; Lula Bannister, piano; Godfrey Wells, Earl Wells, saxaphones. Back row: unidentified non-employee, trombone; Cecil Bannister, trumpet; unidentified non-employee, tuba; William Bannister, drums; Percy Downard, trumpet; Dean Egbert.

program "graduates" can now be found in many political and public activities throughout Puget Power's service territory, making for better understanding between the company and the communities it serves.

Another result of the consumer movement was a new emphasis on the needs of special customer groups. Puget Power pioneered programs tailored to handicapped, low-income and elderly customers, and to refugees whose knowledge of English and prior experience with electricity are limited. The company also packaged and distributed nationally the Gatekeeper program, whereby employees are trained to recognize and act on signs of trouble among customers whose age, health or living conditions place them at risk.

The company received numerous regional and national awards for its community involvement, including a White House award, a federal Private Sector Initiative award, the Washington State Governor's Award

Left: Puget Power Consumer Panels tour Electron generating plant, May 1986. These customers give long hours getting to know the company.

Right: Customers with special needs gain from Puget Power's nationally recognized Gatekeeper program. Here, Oak Harbor meter reader John Thompson works with customer Marge Mansfield.

...Now

A new sound for a new age: The Puget Power Band today. From left, front row: Rich Rucker, synthesizer; Kitty Lynch, Jim Klippert, clarinets; Eric Brateng, Tom Eckhart, saxophones. Back row: Alice Wittenberg, baritone horn; Dick Kaehn, Lynn Logen, trombones; Mark Carson, sousaphone; Don Gaines, drummer; Bob Yetter, Bob Myers, trumpets; Rich Lauckhart, cornet.

and King County Municipal League's "Outstanding Company" award. But Puget Power mounted the programs that achieved this recognition not only to be a good citizen, but chiefly because community involvement is an essential part of Puget Power's business strategy: to serve its customer better and more caringly than the competition.

With the growth in the consumer movement, and the clear desire of a new generation of employees to participate in activities that involve them, a need was recognized for reviewing management practices that had grown up through the years. At Puget Power this took the form of an expanded internal planning

program on a "bottom-up" basis. Clearly, if employees were to feel responsible for the company, they needed a way to "buy in" to what the company was proposing — one more "new reality."

The annual Challenge Series race for handicapped children epitomizes Puget Power's community involvement.

Jerry Brown of the Central Customer Information Center checks a customer's records.

Then...

In 1966, the General Office Building, scarcely a decade old, still housed virtually all of Puget Power's corporate headquarters; and Bellevue was a quietly growing Seattle suburb.

Toward the Future

Speculating on Puget Power's next 100 years, you cannot help being struck with a sense of deja vu. Today deregulation is a mounting trend. The airlines and communication utilities have now seen deregulation, natural gas deregulation is well underway, and quite a body of opinion believes that deregulation in some form will ultimately come to the electric utilities. At the same time electric utilities in many parts of the country are diversifying their activities into non-utility businesses. How similar this sounds to Puget Sound Traction Light & Power Company, Diamond Ice and Storage, the bus company, gas companies,

The diversification trend of the '80s may herald a return to the style of earlier days, when utilities held a variety of businesses. Diamond Ice & Storage Co. was a subsidiary of Puget Power until 1977.

...Now

Today, Bellevue's growth boom has made it one of Washington's largest cities, and Puget Power's headquarters has expanded to occupy several floors in One Bellevue Center, the skyscraper just a block east of the General Office Building.

coal companies, and all of those other activities that were operated in conjunction with the electric utility business many years ago!

Equally interesting is the movement to consolidate utility operations into larger, more efficient units. Some utilities plan to separate their generating and transmission function from their distribution function and to combine the generating and transmission function into a single large organization — much as Charles Baker's Seattle-Tacoma Power Company did many years ago.

Hard as the future may be to predict, these and other trends seem to be the dominant ones. Expanded emphasis on combinations of utili-

Emblematic of the diversification of earlier days is this shot of Puget Power's Bellingham office in 1927, adorned with an ad for a gas subsidiary, and providing a back-drop for the Pacific Northwest Traction Company's Seattle-Bellingham interurban.

**Courtesy of the
U of W Libraries**

Then...

The intersection of 34th and Fremont, in Seattle, was a major crossroads for the electric railways that networked the region during the early 20th century.

Courtesy of the Museum of History & Industry

ties will, no doubt, occur. Expansion into subsidiary and deregulated activities also will happen. To the extent the country moves toward a philosophy more sympathetic to private-ownership, deregulation will certainly expand.

Other fascinating potentials are appearing. Electrical transmission is really still in its infancy, with large losses incurred between generator and user. Recent breakthroughs in cryogenics promise extraordinary efficiency in the movement of electrical energy. The same principles could well lead to more efficient motors and other electrical devices. The smaller-sized generating unit is now with us: The fuel cell, coal gasification, fluidized bed coal generation — these and other technologies will become commonplace. Controls enabling people to use the electrical systems in their homes for a myriad of tasks from energy conservation to connections to computing networks are now in the first stage of implementation.

For Puget Power, the future is full of promise. The company serves a region whose growth potential is extraordinary as a world trade hub. With the advent of expanded transmission, markets for the purchase and sale of electrical energy, from British Columbia to the north, into the Pacific Southwest, are accessible to the company. The only limitations

Energy efficiency became paramount in the '80s. Kevin Beck, Puget Power energy management engineer, shows superintendent Jim Nicholas how to cut energy use at the

U.S. Postal Service Bulk Mail Center, Federal Way.

...Now

The rails are still there, underneath the black-top, at 34th and Fremont today ... and the intersection is dominated by a reminder of its past: Richard Beyer's popular sculpture "Waiting for the Interurban."

may be the boundaries of our own imaginations.

The accelerating rate of technological change makes any precise forecast of business activities too speculative to be worthwhile. But a detached scan of the first century of experience yields a few observations that should apply in any century. The question is, "What was important?" At those crucial turning points when the company's future hung by a thread, what was of greatest concern to those people most able to influence that future?

Light at the end of the tunnel: Looking south through the main pressure tunnel, Baker River hydro project, 1925.

Then...

Playing as hard as they worked, this Puget Power girls' baseball team beat the officials of the Seattle Electric Company at a company picnic in 1911. From left, seated: Sarah McCabe, H.M. Winter (umpire), Bertha Fisher. Standing: Olive Croxford, Hattie Schultz, Winifred Gooch, Ethel Stover, Grace Neal, Ella Falgien, Olga Buse, Valerie LaFortune.

An adequate power supply and a reliable distribution system remain basic to the industry, of course. But it's worth noting that none of the critics of Puget Power during the past century voiced dissatisfaction with the quantity or quality of electric service. Further, despite the efforts to trumpet the rate advantages of public power agencies, the resurrection of the "lively corpse" in 1953 had nothing to do with the price of electricity. Of greater importance have always been a sense of company fairness (the streetcar sale to Seattle was a low point), a perception of good overall value received (the "lively corpse" editorial said it best), and a dem-

onstrated awareness of and responsiveness to customers.

No matter what changes have come to Puget Power and to the industry of which it is a part, nor what changes still await, three elements remain fundamental: the customer, the investor, the employee.

High among corporate priorities must always be listening to the customers as well as talking to them, learning what they expect, what they need, what they think is important. The overhasty dismissal of any customer opinion, however erroneously based, is fraught with peril in the extreme. The unattended matter that seems least important to those

too myopically engaged in day-to-day company business just might be the one to ignite aggrieved customers' passions to the point of triggering disastrous political action. Listening is a matter not only of courtesy and of good citizenship, but of corporate survival.

From the investor perspective, it is critical (as it was in 1953) that the company continue to exist and to remain financially stable. We've found the roots of Puget Power in Sidney Mitchell's Seattle Electric Light Company, and have witnessed dramatic changes over the company's first Century of Service. By the year 2086, the company may be altered even more dramatically, whether through

...Now

Puget Power's 1980 women's softball team. From left, front row: Pat Smith, Mary Moe, Jill Coates, Gail Radtke, Karen Kelly, Susan Guidry, Ellen Torrance, Chris Heaton. Back row: Nick Gullekson (coach), Bonnie Lindner, Louise Wiles, Cindy Keaton, Rick Lindner (coach), Jane Galliher, Ann Goldenberger, Kathy Kosmach, Tom Fournier (coach), Cindy Bunnell, Bill Wood (coach), Karen Sharp.

The Weidemanns: one of many third generation Puget Power families.

Alf Weidemann (1885-1950), son of a Norwegian sea captain, emigrated to the United States in 1904, and joined Stone & Webster in 1910. He served Puget Power's Northern Division as credit manager from 1926 until he retired in 1950.

Earl Myatt came to Puget Power in 1920 after service with the War Department. From the '40s until he retired in 1957, he was Northern Division right-of-way agent. Myatt died in 1979.

Brent Weidemann, grandson of Alf Weidemann and Earl Myatt, remembers accompanying Myatt to look over land purchases as a boy in the '40s. Today, Weidemann is superintendent of substation operations for Northern Division. His son, Timothy Weidemann, is a maintenance man at White River hydroelectric project.

deregulation, diversification, or other industry trends not yet perceptible on the horizon. But it must not become like the legendary hatchet with which George Washington chopped down the cherry tree, which remained unchanged except for two new heads and three new handles. Puget Power must and will remain recognizably responsive to its broad-based owners, who have put not just their money but their faith and trust in the company. They deserve the assurance that corporate assets are well cared for and profitably managed. Only with that assurance can shareholders be expected to fend off unfriendly takeover propositions like those of the early 1950s.

But finally, the resource most critical to the company's survival through its perilous first century has been an ever-present body of dedicated, energetic, well-trained employees. Today, second- and even third-generation Puget Power employees can be found in the company's ranks. The traditions of service, quality and loyalty pass down the line, and are bolstered by the addition of new talents, skills and perceptions from outside.

It's this employee resource that will surely equip the company to meet the challenges of its second century of service. We see the measure of that future already, and step forward to meet it with equally measured paces. The energy starts here.

Brent, July 1987

Tim at work.

PUGET SOUND POWER & LIGHT COMPANY

*Though public takeovers eroded Puget Power's service area
from the 19 counties served in 1940 [See map, page 49], the
nine counties the company serves today include some of the
fastest-growing communities in the nation.*

WHATCOM

SKAGIT

ISLAND

CLALLAM

SNOHOMISH

JEFFERSON

CHELAN

KITSAP

DOUGLAS

MASON

KING

GRAYS
HARBOR

KITTITAS

GRANT

PIERCE

THURSTON

LEWIS

PACIFIC

COWLITZ

W A S H I N G T O N

CLARK

☐ Puget Power Service Area, 1986

O R E G O N

Bibliography

Fun and games at the 1914 company picnic, Puget Sound Traction, Light & Power Co.

As an investor-owned publicly-regulated utility, Puget Power is required to prepare and file voluminous periodic reports of its operations to many local, state, regional and federal authorities. All of this material was available to the editors of this book. Additional references used in preparing the manuscript include the following selected bibliography.

Baker, Charles H., *Life and Character of William Taylor Baker*, New York: The Premier Press, 1908

Kramer, Arthur, *Among the Livewires*, Edmonds, WA: Creative Communications Publishing, 1986

Lee, Kai N. and Donna Lee Klemka with Marion E. Marts, *Electric Power and the Future of the Pacific Northwest*, Seattle: University of Washington Press, 1980

Mitchell, Sidney Alexander, *S.Z. Mitchell and the Electrical Industry*, New York: Farrar, Straus & Cudahy, 1960

Morgan, Lane and Murray Morgan with Paul Dorpat, *Seattle — A Pictorial History*, Norfolk: The Donning Company, 1982

Swett, Ira L., *The Puget Sound Electric Railway — Interurbans Special 23*, Seattle: Interurbans, 1960

Thompson, Wilbur and Allen Beach, *Steamer to Tacoma*, Bainbridge Island, Washington: Driftwood Press, 1963

Turbeville, Daniel E. III, *The Electric Railway Era in Northwest Washington*, 1890-1930, Bellingham, WA: Western Washington University, 1979

Warren, James R., *Seattle — An Illustrated History*, Woodland Hills, CA: Windsor Publications, Inc., 1981

Employees of Puget Power's Western District meet for a picnic on Hood Canal in August, 1927. One of the sporting events was a game called "box Pugets," whose rules are lost in antiquity.

Index

This contemporary line crew from Puget Power's Renton Service Center is a far cry from the Seattle Electric Company's horse-drawn rig and team shown opposite the Preface, pg. 1. Pictured from left: Gerald (Gerry) Schwendeman, line foreman; Chuck Mill, line equipment operator; Richard Munoz (in bucket) and Norman Johnson, linemen.

Photography Index

178